Edward Greey

**Young Americans in Japan**

Edward Greey

**Young Americans in Japan**

ISBN/EAN: 9783337170912

Printed in Europe, USA, Canada, Australia, Japan

Cover: Foto ©ninafisch / pixelio.de

More available books at **www.hansebooks.com**

# THE ROUNDABOUT BOOKS

1. DRIFTING ROUND THE WORLD.
2. A VOYAGE IN THE SUNBEAM.
3. OUR BOYS IN INDIA.
4. OUR BOYS IN CHINA.
5. YOUNG AMERICANS IN JAPAN.
6. YOUNG AMERICANS IN TOKIO.
7. YOUNG AMERICANS IN YEZO.
8. THE FALL OF SEBASTOPOL.
9. FIGHTING THE SARACENS.
10. THE YOUNG COLONISTS.

JAPANESE HOUSE CLEANING.

# THE ROUNDABOUT BOOKS

## YOUNG AMERICANS IN JAPAN

BY
### EDWARD GREEY

AUTHOR OF
"YOUNG AMERICANS IN TOKIO"
"YOUNG AMERICANS IN YEZO"
"BLUEJACKETS" ETC

ILLUSTRATED

BOSTON,
CHARLES E. BROWN & CO.

# PREFACE.

TWENTY-SEVEN years ago an armed fleet "thundered at the gates of Japan," and, in the name of humanity, requested that its harbors should "be opened to the distressed ships of Western nations." I was a member of that expedition, and heard the haughty reply of the official, which was thus interpreted:

"Return from whence you came. No foreigner is permitted to land on our sacred soil!"

How we received this command is a matter of history.

When I first landed in Japan, the feudal system was in full force; the Mikado (Emperor) was virtually a prisoner in Kioto, and none of his subjects were allowed to leave the country. To-day the Mikado rules the land, moves among his subjects like a Western monarch, and is seeking, by every means, to elevate the condition of his people. Japanese merchants are doing business in the principal cities of the world, her earnest students are to be found in our great colleges, and her art illuminates our homes, and has won the admiration of all nations.

Before the first treaty was signed, our ships visited Yezo, and for some time cruised in Japanese waters. I thus had an opportunity of seeing the islands, and of becoming thoroughly acquainted with the coast. At a later period, I returned to the country, lived among its estimable people, studied their language and literature, and, what they term, "learned their hearts."

This book describes the adventures of an American family and a young Japanese who has been educated in the States. They land at Nagasaki, proceed overland to Kokura, cross the strait to Shimonoseki, remain awhile in the province of Nagato, sail up the Inland Sea to Tokio, visit some of its celebrated places, and enjoy the delights of the New Year's festivities, conducted in the olden style.

In Johnnie, Fitz, and Sallie Jewett I have endeavored to depict the keen intelligence of our rising generation; in Oto Nambo, the modern Japanese, who, in adopting Western civilization, has abandoned the traditions of his forefathers; in Mr. and Mrs. Nambo and their friends, the old conservatives who consider the telegraph an invention of demons.

The story, though essentially a work of fiction, is founded on facts that have come under my personal observation, and is intended to make young Americans better acquainted with their good neighbors who inhabit the "Land of the Rising Sun," and to show that all the world is more or less akin, and that wherever the human soul is planted, though obscured by manners and customs the opposite of our own, it bears the stamp of the Divine Image.

EDWARD GREEY.

江戸和留度 偶利君

MANCHESTER-BY-THE-SEA,

# CONTENTS.

| CHAPTER | | PAGE |
|---|---|---|
| I. | AN UNEXPECTED VISITOR | 1 |
| II. | LANDING IN JAPAN | 14 |
| III. | SIGHTS OF NAGASAKI | 33 |
| IV. | NAGASAKI BY NIGHT | 47 |
| V. | KILLING TIME AT AN INN | 62 |
| VI. | FAREWELL TO NAGASAKI | 86 |
| VII. | A PLEASANT JOURNEY | 104 |
| VIII. | OTO'S MANLY AVOWAL | 133 |
| IX. | FROM SHIMONOSEKI TO YOKOHAMA | 161 |
| X. | YOKOHAMA | 170 |
| XI. | TOKIO | 187 |
| XII. | SCENES IN THE CAPITAL | 213 |
| XIII. | THE TEMPLE OF KUWANNON AT ASAKUSA | 231 |
| XIV. | FROM TOKIO TO KANASAWA | 248 |
| XV. | THE GREAT BRONZE IMAGE OF BUDDHA | 264 |
| XVI. | JAPANESE NEW YEAR'S FESTIVITIES | 281 |

# ILLUSTRATIONS.

| | PAGE |
|---|---|
| House-cleaning at Mr. Kingen's. | |
| | *Frontispiece* |
| The Japanese Doll's arrival in America | 1 |
| Otto Nambo | 3 |
| Nambo's Honored Father | 7 |
| Otto's Daimio | 8 |
| Dai koku-fuku-jin | 10 |
| Japanese Pilot Boat | 15 |
| The Island of Decima | 17 |
| A Street in Nagasaki | 19 |
| A Dealer in Sandals | 21 |
| A *Kago* (litter) | 22 |
| Old-clothes Vender | 23 |
| A Blacksmith | 24 |
| Portuguese Bridge, Nagasaki | 25 |
| *Norimono* (enclosed litter) and Bearers | 26 |
| Rope-maker | 27 |
| Toy-maker | 28 |
| Toys representing the God Daruma | 29 |
| Woman Spinning | 30 |
| A Miniature Garden | 31 |
| Interior of Sleeping-Apartment | 32 |
| Kitchen-maid | 34 |
| Buddhist Temple, Nagasaki | 39 |
| Buddhist *Bozu* (ministers) at Prayer | 41 |
| Service in the Buddhist Temple | 43 |
| Picture of Buddhist Last Judgment | 45 |
| The Sick Landlord and the Quacks | 48 |
| The Game of "Catching the Fox" | 51 |
| A Peripatetic Astronomer | 53 |
| Shadows on the Wall | 54 |

| | PAGE |
|---|---|
| Playing Cards | 55 |
| A Famous Singer | 57 |
| Night Watchman | 58 |
| Applying the Moxa | 60 |
| The Golden River | 63 |
| The Japanese Signs for the Hours | 65 |
| Herons and small Birds | 66 |
| Badger on a Bamboo | 67 |
| Geese, Swallows, and Kingfisher | 68 |
| Mekura-hinin, Blind Beggars | 68 |
| Playing the *Koto* (harp) | 69 |
| Master Schiuichiro and his Nurse | 70 |
| A Palmister and his Customers | 73 |
| Drug-store | 75 |
| An Engraver of Pipes | 79 |
| A Peddler of Salt | 80 |
| Performing Boys | 82 |
| Sleeping Women | 84 |
| Smoking Apparatus | 85 |
| Bell Tower | 87 |
| Hideyoshi, likewise called Taiko-Sama | 90 |
| Giving Alms for the Benefit of the Dead | 92 |
| A Visit of Condolence | 93 |
| Reaping the Rice Crop | 94 |
| Cutting Rice | 95 |
| Buddhist Funeral Services | 96 |
| Burning a Body | 98 |
| At the Ancestral Tombs | 99 |
| The Fan Dance | 102 |
| A *Yadoya* (inn) | 105 |

## ILLUSTRATIONS.

| | PAGE | | PAGE |
|---|---|---|---|
| A Gossiping Coolie | 108 | Oto's Foster-Mother, Mitsuro (Mrs. Beeswax) | 199 |
| Tattooed *Betto* (grooms) | 109 | The Indignant Noble | 202 |
| A Girdle Dyer | 110 | A Daimio and his Retainers | 205 |
| Woman Bowing Cotton | 111 | *Rouins* in Ambush | 206 |
| Sawing Timber | 112 | A Soldier of Old Japan | 207 |
| Shinto Temples | 113 | An Allegorical Picture | 208 |
| Shinto Priest and Priestess | 116 | A Japanese Caricature | 209 |
| Ainos from Yezo | 118 | Izakura | 216 |
| Battledoor and Shuttle | 119 | The Great Fish Market of Tokio | 219 |
| A Primitive Scare-crow | 121 | The Venders of Cuttle-fish | 220 |
| A Farmer and his Family | 122 | Cattle-market | 221 |
| A Bird-rattle | 123 | The Lion of the Corea Dancing | 223 |
| Charcoal-seller and Wood-cutter | 123 | The Lion Refreshing Himself | 226 |
| Blessing the Water | 125 | Street Acrobats | 228 |
| Shimonoseki from the heights of Kokura | 127 | A Sword-trick | 234 |
| Town of Shimonoseki | 128 | The Avenue of Asakusa | 235 |
| The Ruins of the Forts of Shimonoseki | 129 | Acrobats | 237 |
| A Passenger Boat | 131 | Distributing Charms, Porch of the Temple of Kuwannon | 241 |
| A Japanese Junk | 132 | Night Scene Outside the Temple | 247 |
| The Long Flight of Steps | 136 | A Japanese Cemetery | 249 |
| The *Torii* at the Landing-place | 137 | The Festival of Yorimitsu | 253 |
| Bozu taking Exercise | 140 | Fuku-roku-jin (Longevity God) | 255 |
| Bozu at Dinner | 142 | A Circulating Library | 256 |
| Oto's Uncle | 143 | A Lantern-maker | 260 |
| Kato Kiyomasa | 145 | A Shinto Ceremony | 262 |
| Japanese Cook's Fan | 147 | The Pagoda and Treasury of the Temple of Hachiman | 266 |
| Festival in Honor of Takenouchi | 149 | Approach to the Temple of Hachiman Kamakoura | 268 |
| A Street Performance | 152 | Terrace of the Temple of Hachiman | 269 |
| A Conjuror | 153 | View of the Island of Enoshima | 271 |
| A Dealer in Bronzes | 154 | Statue of Dai-Butsu (Great Buddha) | 273 |
| The Faithful Lovers of the Takasago Pine | 156 | View of Lake Hakone | 279 |
| A Wedding Ceremony | 157 | *Jin-riki-sha Man* on a Cold Day | 282 |
| Monkey Peak | 159 | Mob before a *Saké* Shop | 285 |
| The Village of Soft-Water | 160 | Embossing Visiting Cards | 286 |
| Pavilion of Sanuki | 162 | Welcoming the New Rice | 287 |
| Fishing by Torchlight | 166 | *Mochi*-makers | 289 |
| Yokohama from the Bluff | 171 | A Poet at Work | 290 |
| Japanese Builders at Work | 173 | New Year's Presents | 292 |
| A Foreign Dog and its Attendant | 174 | The *Maimio* and *Hatamoto* | 293 |
| A Chinese Clerk | 175 | The Ceremony of *Oniwa Soto* | 294 |
| A Curio Store | 177 | The Little Girls' Festival | 297 |
| The Benten *Tori* (avenue) and *Torii* | 179 | Song-sellers in the Street | 300 |
| The Goddess Benten | 180 | *Eta* Dancers | 303 |
| The Gateway of Mr. Nambo's Establishment | 190 | Streets of Tokio, New Year's Afternoon | 305 |
| O-Kiku (Miss Chrysanthemum) | 192 | Modern Japanese | 307 |
| Mr. Nambo's Home | 193 | Fox marked "*Owari*" (The End) | 308 |
| Ruins of a Gateway | 197 | | |

# YOUNG AMERICANS IN JAPAN

THE JAPANESE DOLL'S ARRIVAL IN AMERICA.

# YOUNG AMERICANS IN JAPAN

## CHAPTER I.

### AN UNEXPECTED VISITOR.

*Many a shaft, at random sent,
Finds mark the archer little meant.* — HUDIBRAS.

ONE glorious afternoon in September, two boys and a little girl were earnestly engaged in the walled garden at the rear of their home, putting the finishing touches to a strange-looking instrument that the elder of the lads had constructed out of an old pump-stock.

"I guess this will do," he observed, as he snapped the trigger. "Now if any more of those tramps dare to enter our premises we will give them a dose of cucumbers."

"A dose of what, Johnnie?" inquired his sister Sallie, a dark-eyed child of nine. "What do you mean?"

"We're going to load our cannon with those yellow-skins," answered her brother Fitz, speaking for Johnnie, who was busy with his apparatus. "Won't the tramps run when they find our shot flying about their ears?"

"Bet they will," murmured John, as he pointed the muzzle of the machine toward the door in the garden-wall. "If the selectmen of this place cannot manage the tramps, we will."

The weapon was an ingenious affair, furnished with a spring that threw any light substance, such as a young squash or a ripe cucumber, several yards, and was the result of much thought on the part of its inventor.

Sallie watched Johnnie fire the cannon, and as he sent the missives "bash" against the door, clapped her hands and cried, "Oh, how splendid!"

"Yes," he proudly returned; "I'm thinking of asking papa to take out a patent on this. 'There's millions in it!' 'Jewett's Tramp Terror' would look well in print. Come, Fitz, more ammunition."

Fitz rammed the spring home with a broom-handle, and then picking up a mellow-looking vegetable, inserted the charge in the mouth of the gun. As he did so, some one knocked on the door; but the youngsters being much interested in their amusements, did not hear the summons.

"Try a shot, Sallie," urged Johnnie, offering his sister the trigger-line.

"Oh, I'm afraid!" she said.

"Afraid!" shouted Fitz. "What a coward you are, Sallie; why, it's as easy as anything. Give the line a jerk, the trigger is released, and whiz goes the cucumber. Oh, it's jolly fun!"

The little girl still hesitated; noticing which, Johnnie said, in a coaxing tone, "Oh, Sallie, don't be afraid; this isn't like a real gun; it won't kick."

While her brothers were persuading her, the person at the garden-door knocked a second time. This summons was also unnoticed, Sallie having advanced to the rear of the cannon and timidly taken the line from her elder brother.

"Sister!" cried Fitz, "don't shut both your eyes; if you do, you will never be able to hit a tramp. Come, give the line a pull. Jemmy! — what cowards you girls are!"

This taunt put Sallie on her mettle, and, after tightening the line, she jerked it smartly and released the trigger.

At the same instant the applicant for admission raised the latch, and throwing open the door entered the garden.

"Whiz — bash!" went the cucumber, striking the lintel and scattering the seeds all over the intruder.

"My!" ejaculated Sallie, starting back with affright. "What's that?"

"Hello — are you a tramp?" cried Fitz, gaping at their victim.

"Goodness!" gasped Johnnie. "It's — a — lady!"

The cause of their amazement was a pale-faced, gentle-looking individual, dressed in a white robe, dark petticoat, and wide-sleeved over-garment of silk, who regarded them for an instant, then said, in very excellent English:

"A thousand pardons. Can you inform me where Professor Jewett lives?"

OTO NAMBO.

Johnnie glanced first at his sister, next at his brother, and finally at the speaker; then pointing behind him, replied: —

"Yes, Miss; that is the Professor's house, and we are his children."

The stranger gravely brushed off some seeds that had fallen upon his bushy, black hair, and smiling, said:

"I am not a young lady, I am a boy; my name is Oto Nambo."

"Are you a Chinese?" bluntly inquired Fitz.

"No," proudly answered the lad; "I am a Japanese. My countrymen were never conquered by the Tartars. I am afraid I have interrupted your sport."

While he was speaking, Sallie, who felt ashamed of the reception they had given the stranger, hurried toward the house.

Johnnie briefly explained his object in making the cannon; then inquired:

"How came you to enter by the garden door?"

The young Japanese told them that he had been so directed by a woman whom he had met on the street, adding, merrily:

"She evidently took me for a Chinese, and thought I was in the laundry business."

He was so gentlemanly and good-natured that both Johnnie and Fitz took a liking to him right away, and when they had shaken his hand, conducted him indoors to the library, where they found their father engaged in writing.

"Well, sir," inquired the Professor, after he had welcomed the visitor, "what can I do for you?"

Oto produced a letter from the sleeve of his outer garment, and handing the missive to his host, remarked:

"Your brother, Doctor Jewett, of Tokio, was my honored instructor. That note will explain my presence here."

The gentleman opened the envelope and read:

"IMPERIAL HOSPITAL, TOKIO, JAP.
"AUGUST 1, 18—.

"DEAR JOHN:—This is to introduce you to Mr. Oto Nambo, o.. of my pupils, and the son of my good friend Nambo, of whom you h  often heard me speak. Oto desires to study the higher branches chemistry, so I have advised him to visit the States and place hims under your instruction. He is a truly noble, gentle, honorable boy, a  I would much like to hear that he had become an inmate of your fam I have known Oto from his childhood, and feel as much regard for l as though he were a relative. Give him a hearty welcome, for the s?! of your brother,
"FITZGERALD JEWET:.

"P. S.—Remember me affectionately to your wife, and to S;.. and the boys."

As the Professor concluded reading this, Mrs. Jewett a her daughter entered the room.

"Ellen," he said, introducing their visitor, "this is Mr. O Nambo, a friend of my brother Fitz."

The hostess and Sallie bowed to the Japanese, who j. foundly returned their salute, and said:

"Ladies, I am delighted to have the happiness of meeti  you. I trust you are both in the enjoyment of good health."

He neither, by word nor look, showed that he had ? viously seen the little girl, who felt truly grateful for consideration.

"He is real good," she thought. "Some boys would l  been mad at having cucumbers fired at them."

After supper the Professor and Mrs. Jewett held a corsu- tation, and that evening they invited Oto to take up his al with them.

"Won't it be jolly?" cried Fitz. "You can teach Japanese, and we'll instruct you in base-ball and lots of th; Say, why do you not wear American clothes?"

"I intend to do so now."

"I thought most of your countrymen did," observed Johnnie.

"All our officials, and many of my friends have adopted Western costume," answered the boy. "I have long desired to do so, but my mother said, No; so I have continued to wear my native dress. When I bade her good-by, she whispered, 'My son, if, on arriving in America, you find it best to wear the costume of the people, I will make no further objection.'"

Mrs. Jewett, who was highly pleased with him, glanced toward Fitz, then said to their guest:

"Do Japanese boys always obey their mothers?"

"Of course, madam," he replied, as though surprised at her question. "Nobody ever thinks of disobeying their parents."

Fitz, who was blushing like a girl, bit his lips, and muttered:

"I'm afraid we American boys are not like you. We try to obey, but sometimes slump up."

"Do what?" quietly inquired Oto.

"He means that he cannot always accomplish his wish," said Mrs. Jewett. "Slump is not a very pretty word to use."

After the gas was lighted, the children asked Oto about his family, whereupon he produced a photograph of his father, and remarked:

"This was taken some years ago, when my honored father was the chief councillor of our *dai-mio* (great lord)."

"How funny," observed Johnnie. "Why did he have the top of his head shaved, and the hair on the sides gathered up into that gun-hammer queue?"

"The custom originated when my warrior countrymen began to wear helmets," answered Oto. "If they had permitted their hair to grow as I do, they could not have worn

NAMBO'S HONORED FATHER.

those metal head-coverings. You will observe my parent has his pipe in his left hand, and his sword on the mat near him. Now the wearing of swords by the nobility and gentry is abolished, and no one is ever seen with them."

"What is that little parcel lying before your father?" inquired Sallie, who took a deep interest in the boy's description. "And what is that tube between the sword and cup?"

OTO'S DAI-MIO.

"The parcel is my father's tobacco-pouch, and what you call a tube is his pipe-case. A Japanese pipe only holds a tiny pinch of tobacco. The vessels on the stand upon my father's right are a tea-pot, a kettle for hot water, and a bowl for tea sediment."

"What is the screen behind him?" asked Johnnie.

"It represents the partition that divided the photographer's studio from his living-room. The picture was not taken in our home."

Oto then showed them another portrait, and said:

"This is the photograph of our *dai-mio* or lord, in his old costume."

"Is that a dunce's cap?" demanded Fitz.

"No," answered Oto; "it was the court head-dress of the *dai-mio*. I can assure you my late lord is anything but a dunce. The robes that appear so strange to you really gave an air of dignity to their wearer."

"Why is he kneeling, and why did he have such long pants?" asked Johnnie.

"He is not kneeling," answered Oto. "It was the custom for our nobles to wear flowing trousers, just as your ladies wore long trains to their dresses."

"We don't now," said Sallie.

"More do we," said Oto. "All those things belong to the past,—to old Japan, when the *shogun* or military power governed my country. Now the mikado (emperor) is the sole ruler, our officials wear foreign uniforms, and our soldiers and sailors are dressed like your own."

"Where did you learn to speak such excellent English?" inquired Fitz.

"In Tokio. I have been studying your language for five years, and am a graduate of the Imperial College."

"Come, children," remarked Mrs. Jewett, "it is growing late. Professor, will you show our guest to his room? Mr. Oto, I have had your chamber made as comfortable as possible."

Oto bade his new friends good-night, and followed his host, who, as they ascended the stairs, said:

"I am sorry we could not give you rice and fish for supper. After this, you shall have them at every meal."

"Oh, I can eat American food," was the quiet rejoinder. "Please do not prepare rice especially for me; I am not so fond of it as you may imagine, and can eat almost anything you do."

When they entered the sleeping-apartment, the Professor pointed to a corner in which some wadded quilts were neatly arranged, and observed:

"This is the best we can do to-night. Mrs. Jewett had the bedstead and furniture removed, and new matting laid, so as to make your room as homelike as possible. We wish you to imagine you are in your own house. There is a bath in the next room, and hot water. Please turn off the gas, and do not blow it out or you will be smothered. If you require any more quilts, ring, and I will send some to you. Good-night."

As the gentleman descended the stairs, Oto smiled, and thought:

"They imagine, because I am a Japanese, I cannot sleep in a bed. How comical! Well, as they have taken all this trouble to strip the apartment, and make it homelike for me, I'll not undeceive them."

Thus thinking, he went to his trunk, and, after searching awhile, discovered a paper bearing a representation of *Dai-koku* (the god of luck). This he laughingly affixed to the wall; having done which, he made up the quilts Japanese fashion, as bed and bed-clothes, and retired for the night.

DAI-KOKU FUKU-JIN.

The next morning, Fitz entered the room and announced that breakfast was almost ready; then, as he regarded the picture of the god, said:

"Hello! who is that?—another relative of yours?"

Oto's eyes twinkled, as he replied:

"No; that is Dai-koku fuku-jin. Your good parent has kindly endeavored to render my room like that of a Japanese, so I have completed the illusion by adding a picture of the god of luck, which was slipped into my trunk by dear old Mitsu-ro, my foster-mother."

"*Day-cookyou* is a comical-looking critter," said Fitz, grinning at the picture; "tell me something about him. Who was he, anyhow?"

Oto laughed heartily, and answered:

"Dai-koku, who is by foreigners termed the god of wealth, or luck, was the son of Sos-anu-no-mikoto. He is a very popular deity in my country, and is always represented as standing on two bales of rice, with a sack of money on his back. In his right hand he holds a miner's hammer, signifying: 'if you would have lots of money in your bag and rice in your storeroom, you must work for it as a miner does with his tools.'"

"He's awfully homely, isn't he?" mused Fitz.

"Yes," chuckled Oto. "We do not consider him very handsome. Still, many of my countrymen and women venerate him, and make offerings before his picture."

"Say, Oto, you don't believe in any such nonsense, do you? Why do you keep that thing? It is idolatrous."

The Japanese boy laughed, and replied:

"Oh! I have no faith in Dai-koku; I merely put him there to carry out your good mother's idea. You will find such a picture in nearly all our houses."

When Fitz related the foregoing conversation to his mother, she thought for a while, then said to her husband:

"Professor, I believe Oto would like an American bed; he is too proud to acknowledge his people's way of sleeping is not as comfortable as ours."

"Yes, I agree with you, wife; we will treat this young Japanese just as we would an American guest. It is amazing how readily his countrymen adopt our ways."

After a good breakfast, during which Oto showed a thorough appreciation of American beefsteak and buckwheat cakes, and did not ask for rice, the boys conducted him to a clothing store, where he purchased a hat and an excellent outfit. This done, he had his hair cut, and on his return, when he donned his new garments, he looked as neat and nice as either of his friends. On discovering that the furniture had been restored to his room, he took down the picture of Dai-koku, remarking, with a merry laugh:

"This was never intended to ornament an American apartment. I will not destroy it, as it was the last gift of my good old Mitsu-ro, but will pack it away with my *kimono* (long robe) and *hakama* (trousers). Now I am in America I am going to be an American."

From that day he became like one of the family, and by his gentleness of manner, decision of character, nobility of nature, and general amiability, made numerous friends in Cromlech.

He taught his host, hostess, and their children to speak, read, and write Japanese; and entering the college of which the Professor was one of the faculty, passed his examinations with credit to himself and instructors.

One evening, five years after Oto's arrival in the States, the Professor said to his family:

"I have been thinking of going to Japan with Oto, and of making a tour through the country. What do you say to it?"

"If we can accompany you, Yes," answered Mrs. Jewett. "Johnnie, Fitz, and Sallie would thoroughly enjoy the trip, and I would much like to visit 'The Land of the Rising Sun.'"

At first the Professor demurred, saying it would cost too much. However, upon making a calculation, he agreed to take them, remarking:

"You will understand one thing: we are to go by sailing-ship, and upon our arrival in the country to endeavor to live in Japanese fashion. We will land in the south at Nagas-aki, and travel inland through Hizen and Chikuzen, cross the strait to Shimonoseki, embark on board a native steamer, and proceed up the Inland Sea to Tokio, where we will remain six months."

"Hurrah!" cried Johnnie and Fitz.

"Isn't it splendid?" said Sallie. "Oh, I do so want to visit Japan."

"Yes, I like the idea vastly," observed her mother. "What do you say, Oto?"

"I think you will have a good time, see lots of interesting places and things, and learn all about my countrymen and women," answered the Japanese. "Your decision makes me very happy."

On the first of March, the Professor, his wife, family, and friend were on their way to the far East.

## CHAPTER II.

### LANDING IN JAPAN.

*They sailed away for a far-off strand,
And for weeks and weeks never sighted land.* — MILLER.

THE "Northern Star," which carried the Jewetts to Japan, was a slow-sailing ship, and it was not until daybreak of the first of July that the look-out man announced:

"Land on our port-bow!"

"Hurry up, Fitz! — hurry up, Oto! Come, Sallie, and father and mother," shouted Johnnie, who was on deck when the sailor made the discovery. "Turn out and see the glorious land of the Rising Sun."

It did not take them very long to make their toilets, and as the mist cleared away, and the golden orb rose from its bed in the East, the family mustered on deck and saw right ahead a line of blue mountains clearly defined on the Western horizon. Johnnie, Fitz, and Oto mounted the rigging, and ensconced themselves in the fore-top, while the Professor, his wife, and daughter took their places abaft on the poop.

The boys had grown fine manly fellows, — Johnnie being sixteen, Fitz thirteen, and Oto nineteen. They were all strong, active, and intelligent, and could speak, read, and write Japanese as well as they could English and French.

Sallie had developed into a charming miss, and was fourteen years old. She, like her brothers, was well versed in Japanese, in addition to which she could play on a *samisen* (Japanese guitar), which Oto had imported for her.

"Oh, I am so glad!" she exclaimed, as she glanced at the

distant land. "I do so want to have a run on shore. Papa, I hope you will take us home by steamer."

"Deck ahoy!" shouted Johnnie, who was quite a sailor. "There's a queer-looking canoe coming off to us."

"Ay, ay, my son, I see her," bawled the captain; "it is a pilot-boat."

As the vessel had a fair wind, and the approaching craft was vigorously rowed by four stout Japanese, they soon neared

JAPANESE PILOT-BOAT.

one another, when the "Northern Star" was hove-to, and a rope thrown to their visitor.

The pilot, a sturdy Japanese, dressed in native costume, clambered up the ship's side, and after shaking everybody by the hand, as though they were old friends, ordered his boat to be made fast astern, and took charge of the ship.

He was delighted to find the passengers could speak Japanese, and divided his time between directing the vessel and chatting with the boys.

As they drew near to the shore, he excused himself from further conversation, remarking that the navigation was somewhat dangerous, and he must attend solely to his duty.

Fortunately for the voyagers, the wind remained fair; so in tnree hours they were inside the headland, and tacking up the picturesque Bay of Nagasaki.

"See yonder island," said Oto, who knew every spot they passed. "That is Pappenberg, the rock from which, in 1637, thousands of Christians were hurled."

"What brutes your countrymen must have been," observed Johnnie.

"Yes; they were not noted for their gentleness to those who did not believe in their faith," he quietly answered. "If I remember rightly, some of your own people were, at a later date, not much more considerate of Quakers and the so-called witches."

"That's so," said Sallie. "You do not persecute Christians now, do you?"

"Far from it," returned Oto. "We not only permit missionaries to settle all over the country, but we have abolished the edict boards that were formerly erected at the entrance to every village."

"What were these?"

"They were official notices, forbidding any one to embrace the faith of the foreigner. Now our people can believe whatever their conscience tells them is right. I referred to the massacre of my Christian countrymen in order to show you what wonderful changes have taken place in Japan."

While they were conversing, a tug-boat, flying the flag of the country, — a red ball (sun) on a white ground, — came steaming out of the inner harbor, and when the health-officer had boarded the ship and granted her *pratique*, the "Northern Star" was made fast to the tiny craft, which proceeded to tow her at a high rate of speed.

"That boat was built in Nagasaki, by Japanese, and her engines and boilers are of native manufacture," proudly remarked the pilot. "You see we are going ahead like Americans."

As they neared their anchorage, they noticed a low island thickly studded with warehouses.

"Yonder is Decima," said Oto. "It was there that, for over two hundred years, the Dutch were permitted to live.

THE ISLAND OF DECIMA.

Singularly enough, at one time, it was the only spot in the world where their flag was flying, the Hollanders having been temporarily conquered by a more powerful nation."

The boys took a hurried glance at the interesting island, then commenting upon the obstinacy of the Dutch character, went below to prepare for landing.

Within half an hour the anchor was dropped in the deep water, and the Jewetts embarked in a native boat and were landed on the custom-house wharf.

When their baggage and passports had been slightly examined by the customs' officials, who all wore foreign uniforms, they were asked whether they desired to go to the English or native hotel.

The Professor said, "to the Japanese;" whereupon their effects were taken in charge by an expressman, who wore only one cotton garment, and had his head tied about with a towel. After the man had started, the Professor and his party walked leisurely toward the inn.

"What narrow streets!" remarked Sallie. "There are no windows to the stores, and the houses are all open in front."

"Yes," said Oto. "You will not find stores here like those at home."

"Isn't this your home?" slily inquired Johnnie.

"Well, I meant in the States," merrily answered their friend.

They proceeded through the main street, which was paved in the centre, and kept beautifully clean and neat.

Few of the houses were more than one-story high, and none of them were remarkable for architectural beauty.

"Our dwellings are built to live in, not to look at," said Oto.

"Why is the hill at the back of the city cut into steps?" inquired Sallie.

"It is terraced for the purpose of keeping the soil from washing down into the valley," said Oto. "We have such a large population that every inch of ground has to bear its crop."

"What is that two-storied place, with heavy tiled eaves," asked Johnnie.

"A temple."

"Are there any foreign churches here?"

"Yes, there are several in and about Nagasaki, and a large

A STREET IN NAGASAKI.

number in the capital and open ports. I saw, by a recent copy of the 'Tokio Times,' that it is estimated there are thirty-five thousand Christians in Japan."

After walking quite a distance, they arrived at a neatly-kept and extensive establishment on Eastern Ocean Street.

"Remember," whispered Oto, "you must not enter a Japanese house with your shoes on. The waitresses will bring you tubs of water in which to lave your feet, and you must not be astonished at the proprietor kneeling, bowing his head to the ground, and making very humble apologies for the poorness of the accommodations. The latter you will find good enough."

"Then why will he apologize?" demanded Fitz.

"Because it is our custom," said Oto.

On reaching the entrance to the inn, they were met by a smiling landlady, dressed in gray garments, who, prostrating herself in the veranda, murmured in Japanese, —

"I fear my house will afford you very miserable accommodation."

The Professor said something polite in return, and when the party had removed their shoes, they entered, and were conducted to a suite of apartments in the back of the house.

"Why," cried Fitz, "there are no rooms in this place. It is one big hall, partitioned off with screens. I want to have a chamber that overlooks the street."

The landlady led him into a side apartment, and drawing back a shutter, said, —

"There is the street, sir, outside. We desire to furnish you with everything you wish."

Oto ordered a meal to be prepared, and the travellers retired to their respective quarters, the boys being allotted one room, which was simply a matted space inclosed with beautifully-decorated screens.

"No beds, no chairs, no tables, no stools, no fireplaces, no washbowls," grumbled Johnnie. "On what are we to sit?"

"On the nice, clean, matted floor," merrily replied Oto. "Now you are in Japan, you must do as we do."

"I want to know," growled the boy. "Well, I guess this is no more strange to us than our country and ways were to you?"

"No," was the laughing response. "We each have our manners and customs. Anyhow, we did not welcome you with a discharge of ripe cucumbers."

A DEALER IN SANDALS.

The boys laughed at this, and seating themselves at the open window, watched the scene in the street.

On the opposite side of the way was a booth, in which straw sandals were exposed for sale. The dealer — a fat, sleepy-looking man — sat on a mat behind his wares, smoking and dozing. When his customers wanted his goods, they helped themselves, and threw down the value, — about two cents a pair.

Most of the purchasers wore straw foot-gear, though some of them were perched on wooden clogs, that made a great clatter on the cobble-stones.

Presently, two men came by, carrying a *Kago* (litter), in which a young girl was doubled up. Her clogs were laid on the top of the apparatus, and the latter was scarcely high enough

A KAGO (LITTER).

to admit of her sitting upright. The bearers halted for a moment, when she turned her pretty face toward the strangers, and glanced at them half-curiously, half-timidly, then bade the men go on.

"She never knew the luxury of a Pullman car," laughingly remarked Johnnie; "how ever can she double herself up in that style."

"You'll have to do it yet," said Oto.

While they were chatting, a man carrying a wooden horse or rack, on which were spread various worn coats and other garments, came along the street, and pausing before the window, deposited his load.

"He is a second-hand-clothes man," said Oto. "Wat him: that woman is after some of his wares."

The customer, who had a baby strapped to her back, advanced, and taking one of the robes, said,—

"How much?"

"A yen (dollar)."

"Oh, impossible."

"Cheap," mumbled the man. "It is as good as new."

OLD-CLOTHES VENDER.

"I'll give you twenty-five *sen* (cents)."

"No; I should lose by it."

"Thirty."

"Couldn't; I'd starve if I sold goods at that rate."

"Fifty *sen;* not a cash more," dropping the robe and turning away.

"Here, take it," said the dealer, sighing; "it is exactly what it cost me."

When the woman had departed with her purchase, the fellow turned to the boys, and, rolling his eyes comically, cried:

"Ah, that was a good sale! I made my day's rice and fish out of her."

"Come," said Fitz; "while father. mother, and Sallie are resting, let us take a walk."

They stepped through the open window, entered the street, and strolled down to a place where they saw a crowd of boys watching a smith making a chain. He was not overburdened with clothes, nor was his assistant, — a villanous-looking youth, who squatted by his side.

The bellows were contained in an upright box, and were blown by the master, who worked the handle with his right

A BLACKSMITH.

foot. Though his tools were few in number and rude in construction, he turned out very neat work.

"Do all your mechanics squat on the ground in that way?" asked Johnnie, as they moved off. "Do none of them ever use a bench, as ours do?"

"Yes; they sometimes work at a low block of wood, raised about four inches from the floor," answered Oto. "My countrymen neither care to stand at meals nor at their occupations, as yours do."

The friends strolled towards the suburbs, nobody taking much notice of them, foreigners being common enough in Nagasaki.

PORTUGUESE BRIDGE, NAGASAKI.

After proceeding some distance, they came to a bridge, which Oto said was built by the Portuguese, and was the only one of the kind in Japan.

"This isn't much of a river to require such a high bridge," remarked Fitz.

"You should see it during the rainy season," returned Oto. "I tell you they want a strong structure then. The water

NORIMONO (ENCLOSED LITTER) AND BEARERS.

comes tumbling down from the hills, bringing stones and trees, and it is a wonder this old bridge has withstood so many floods."

In the midst of their conversation, two men came staggering along, bearing between them a sort of coach, which depended from a heavy beam resting on their shoulders. On arriving at the bridge, they placed bamboo sticks under the beam, lowered it to within a foot of the ground, and began to wipe the perspiration from their brows.

"Are you taking me right?" demanded their passenger, a rather pretty woman. "You ought to have crossed higher up," pointing to the left.

The foremost of the men peeped round at her and said, in a conciliatory tone:

"Honorable wife, we are taking you right. Look at those foreigners; see how they are staring at you."

The lady glanced at the boys, bit her cherry lips, and pulling down the blind of the conveyance, hid herself from view.

"What is that machine?" asked Johnnie.

"That is a *norimono* (enclosed litter)," said Oto. "In the old times only our nobles and gentlefolks, and their ladies, rode in such vehicles; now any one can use them. They are much more comfortable than the *kago*."

They watched the bearers resume their burden and stagger off, then Fitz said,—

"Why don't you use horses instead of men?"

ROPE-MAKER.

"Because human muscle, flesh and blood, are worth less than that of the animals you name," replied the Japanese. "In Tokio you will see men drawing *jin-riki-sha*, — little carriages made to carry one or two persons."

"You would not find an American willing to play horse in that way," remarked Johnnie. "Hello! what is that man doing down there?"

"He is making rope," said Oto. "Come, we will ask him to explain how he does it."

The man, who was polishing cordage with a tar-covered rag, eyed them askance, and continued his work without replying to Oto's inquiry.

Presently the master of the rope-walk appeared, and after saluting them politely, said, —

"That boy of mine is not quite bright; all he knows is how to make rope."

He exhibited a wheel to which the strands were fastened and explained how they were twisted, then observed, —

"Formerly, I made rattan ropes and cotton cordage; now I only manufacture hempen cables for foreign ships."

"What are these tags for?" inquired Fitz, pointing to some slips of wood, branded, —

"ROYAL MILLS, BERMONDSEY, ENGLAND.
WARRANTED ALL HEMP."

"They are supplied to me by the foreign merchant who buys my rope. I do not know what is on them."

When the lads told him, he became very indignant, saying, —

TOY-MAKER.

"I will not use them. I make good rope, and do not wish to have it sold as English. This is how foreigners kill our native trade. I always imagined those labels bore my name and address."

"Now you know," said Johnnie. "Good-day."

They proceeded to the next street, where they halted before a house, in the front room of which sat a man making dolls without legs or arms, — queer-looking things, with comical features.

As he painted the toys, he stuck them into a block of rice-straw, bound with a cord of the same material. He was a merry fellow; and on seeing his visitors, cried, —

"Ah! my lords; want a nice toy to carry home to your family? My Daruma are the best-made articles in Nagasaki, only five *sen* each."

Johnnie purchased one for Sallie, and as he carried it to the inn, asked why it had no legs.

"Daruma was one of Buddha's disciples," slyly answered Oto. "He was so pious, and prayed so continually, that he wore his limbs clean down to his body. In the old times, he was greatly venerated. Now his face, wrapped in tobacco-leaves, is used as a tobacconist's sign, and that rolling toy is made in his image. Our boys always fashion their snow-men after that shape"

TOYS REPRESENTING THE GOD DARUMA.

"Isn't it making fun of him?" suggested Johnnie.

"Of course it is," returned Oto. "We Japanese make fu.. of everything."

The boys returned to the inn, where they found the rest of their party partaking of dinner.

"What sort of a bill of fare is it?" asked Fitz of Sallie, who was doing her best to eat with chop-sticks.

"Oh, it isn't so bad," she replied. "The rice is nice, the soup pretty good, and the fish delicious."

"Yes," nodded the Professor, "it is all well cooked and served, and is very nutritious. Make up your minds to like it, and it is excellent."

After dinner, the ladies went into the kitchen, and were introduced to the daughter of their hostess, who was spinning cotton with an old-fashioned wheel. She worked very rapidly, and talked freely with her visitors, asking a hundred questions concerning America and its people.

WOMAN SPINNING.

"Are you happy?" inquired Mrs. Jewett, who was an advocate of woman's rights.

"Yes," was the laughing reply. "Are you? I have all I want, and what more can I wish?"

Mrs. Jewett did not inquire any further.

They spent the remainder of the day in their room, which overlooked a miniature garden, that their hostess said represented a real scene.

At the back, built against the fence, was a rockery containing a cave, before it being a diminutive image of a goddess. A small bridge crossed the tiny stream, and the latter was alive with frogs that winked and blinked at the foreigners, as though they knew they were strangers.

"I keep this in order myself," remarked their hostess. "If the frogs get into your room, please do not injure them."

A MINIATURE GARDEN.

"I will not," said Mrs. Jewett, who fervently hoped the creatures would remain in their proper quarters.

About nine o'clock, the guests began to retire for the night.

The chamber adjoining the boys', was a large one, in which four young Japanese were accommodated.

These lads were students, and full of fun. "Hello!" cried one of them, addressing Oto. "How are you, my lord. I suppose, because you wear American clothes, and speak the language, you think yourself too good to recognize your old comrade, Ichiro?"

"What!" exclaimed Oto, "are you the little boy I left in Tokio?"

"No; I am the young man you find in Nagasaki," was the bantering response.

Oto was overjoyed to meet his friend, and when he had introduced the Jewett boys, they had a good time.

INTERIOR OF SLEEPING-APARTMENT.

That night they left the screens open between the apartments, and the last thing Johnnie saw was Oto, who, dressed in one of his schoolfellow's robes, was sitting near him, chatting in Japanese, while the three other students were lying prone on the floor, with their shaven heads propped upon wooden pillows, shaped like clogs.

Then, wearied with his first day's experience in Japan, the young American fell asleep.

## CHAPTER III.

### SIGHTS OF NAGASAKI.

> The maids were singing in the kitchen, and
> I heard the shampooers whistling in the street;
> Then I turned over on my mat, and said:
> "I think it is time I arose."— JAPANESE POEM.

AT daybreak Fitz was awakened by the noises of the inn, and a continuous low whistling in the street.

He aroused Oto, who quoted the foregoing poem; adding, —

"Would you like to be shampooed?"

"I would," said Johnnie, opening his eyes. "I want a bath, and to have my hair dressed."

"Our shampooers do not fix one's hair in the American fashion," observed their friend. "They punch, pound, rub, and knead the body, and make you feel as limber as an acrobat. If you would like that, I will go out and secure three of them."

"Go ahead," cried Fitz.

When Oto had departed, Fitz rose, and slipping on his clothes, proceeded to the kitchen for a cup of water.

He found the cooks hard at work boiling huge vessels of rice over small earthen furnaces, the fuel of which was charcoal. Addressing a girl, who was polishing a saucer and singing at the top of her voice, he said, —

"Miss, will you kindly give me some water?"

She stopped short in the midst of an excruciating quaver, and, bowing, replied, —

"Sir, do not drink water; it is bad for you." Then pouring some tea into a porcelain cup, handed it to him, remarking,—

KITCHEN-MAID.

"Your honorable father and mother, and your sister, have gone to the Buddhist temple. They left word with me for you to follow them."

Having said this, she resumed her song, as follows:

"*O-oee oyazo dono so-no-kane
Kochi-raye kashite gun-nan-se.*"

The literal translation of which is,— ᾽

Or, "See here, old gentleman, you must lend me that money."

She screeched this at the top of her voice, quavering each note in such a comical fashion that Fitz could not avoid smiling, — noticing which, she said, —

"My lord, your friend is calling you."

The girl evidently considered herself a first-class singer, and resented his exhibition of merriment.

Fitz returned to his room, where he found three shaven-headed shampooers, clad in white robes. Two of the men were engaged in rubbing and slapping Oto and Johnnie, who, extended on the floor, appeared to enjoy the performance.

"Come, my lord," observed the unoccupied man, advancing with extended hands, and feeling for Fitz; "I am ready to shampoo you."

"Why, you are blind, are you not?" murmured the lad.

"Oh, yes," proudly. "I have been sightless from my birth, but I can see with my fingers. Now, off with your robes, and lie down. I will soon make you think you are in Paradise."

The boy obeyed, and in a few moments was being slapped and kneaded by the shampooer, who, as he worked, laughed and joked in a very merry fashion.

He snapped the joints of the lad's fingers and limbs, rubbed, pounded, and worked at him until Fitz cried, —

"Guess that will do; I feel as though I want to rise and dance. How much do I owe you?"

The blind man closed his eyes, puckered his face into a smile, and bowing, said, —

"My lord, you foreigners always pay what you please."

"I'll settle for this," whispered Oto, giving each man a few *sen*.

The one who had shampooed Fitz ⁀rove of this interference, and became very saucy, saying, in a mocking tone:

"Oh, it is beautiful to go abroad and learn a foreign language. I think I shall send my son to America, then, when he returns, he will warn his friends not to give a poor shampooer more than a hundred cash (ten cents) for his services."

"Yes, yes," satirically chorussed the other men; "we, too, will send our sons abroad to learn how to grind the faces of our countrymen."

"Let us give them a quarter apiece," suggested Johnnie.

"Not a cash more," said Oto. "When I was in the States you would not permit me to be imposed upon."

Turning to the indignant blind man, he cried, —

"Be off, or I will send for the police. I have given each of you more than your proper pay."

Their leader picked up his staff, and, feeling his way out, quitted the room, followed by his companions, all of them grumbling at the top of their voices.

"I paid them enough," remarked Oto. "If you begin by giving foreign prices and remuneration you will have to continue it. How do you feel, boys?"

"Hungry," they answered.

Just then a lad peeped into the room and cried in a shrill tone, —

"*O-mamma! O—h maa——ma!*"

"Your mother isn't here. Go on to the next den," said Johnnie.

Oto smiled.

"*O-mamma!*" again yelled the boy, glancing at Fitz.

"Did not that gentleman tell you that your mamma isn't here?" said Fitz. "Go 'long!"

"Come in, boy," laughingly observed Oto; "I will take some."

In walked the lad, bringing a bucket containing cold rice, some bowls, and a dipper.

He placed the articles on the floor, and served Oto with a ladleful; then handing him a pair of chopsticks, once more addressed the other lads, saying,

"*O-mamma!*"

"Go along," cried Fitz. "Haven't I told you your mother wasn't here? Give me some of that rice, I'm hungry."

"And so am I," said Johnnie; adding, "you are a big fellow to go bawling 'round for your mother."

The waiter, for such was his occupation, did not take any notice of their remarks, but, after serving them, went off yelling his strange cry.

"I suppose this is a sort of breakfast?" said Fitz, as he attacked the food.

"It's *o-mamma*, the vulgar name for boiled rice," merrily responded Oto. "The lad was not calling for his mother!"

"I thought *amma* was the Japanese for a child's nurse," growled Fitz. "Why didn't you tell us what it meant? We never played off such jokes upon you."

Oto's eyes sparkled merrily as he answered, —

"What, never? I remember the first evening I was at your house, when I went to take a bath I found the soap would not lather. I scrubbed and rubbed until I almost took the skin off my body, then discovered the point of your joke. Pardon me if I have permitted you to learn for yourselves that *o-mamma* is not 'where's my mother.'"

They laughed heartily at his gentle revenge, and after they had partaken of the food, set out for the Temple, which was built upon a hill in the outskirts of the city.

The morning sun was well up, and its rays were powerful, so the boys purchased paper umbrellas, and walked slowly.

They crossed a narrow bridge, spanning a shallow stream, and saw that below on their left the water had been led off into a sort of canal to feed an undershot wheel.

"That is a rice-mill," said Oto. "We shall see lots of them during our travels."

"Are there any fish in this stream?" inquired Fitz of a boy who was regarding him with open mouth.

The lad, amazed to hear a foreigner speak his language, nodded, and said,—

"Yes; there's plenty of trout in that water, but you had better not try to catch them. It is owned by Mr. Sixteen-fields, who will not kill anything."

"He must be a very humane man,—a sort of Henry Bergh," said Johnnie.

"Oh, no," answered Oto. "He is only a fanatical Buddhist. They won't even kill flies."

Leaving the mill-wheel plashing, and the mill going "thud—thud—thud!" they ascended a steep street, and soon neared their destination,—a temple dedicated to "The ever Merciful Buddha."

The approach to the building was by a series of stone steps, that showed signs of the wear of millions of sandalled feet. On each side of these flights were low buildings devoted to the sale of charms and rosaries.

"What a curious roof," remarked Johnnie. "The frame of the building must be very strong to support such a weight."

"Yes," answered Oto; "the temple is built of solid beams, hewn out of forest-trees. It has stood many an earthquake."

They ascended the last steps, and entered the enclosure containing the main building of the temple.

"Look at those strange trees," said Fitz "What are they?"

BUDDHIST TEMPLE, NAGASAKI.

"Tree ferns," returned Oto. "They were brought from India, and are considered sacred. What do you think of the porch of the temple?"

His companions glanced at the structure, and Fitz said,—

"It looks top-heavy. Come, I've seen enough of the porch, so let us go inside."

On mounting the temple steps, upon which stood a *bozu* (priest) and five worshippers, they saw the Professor's shoes and those of Mrs. Jewett and Sallie. Having removed their foot-coverings, the lads entered the building and beheld the party squatting upon the matted floor.

"Sesch!" said the Professor, signalling his sons not to make a noise. "Come and sit by us; the *bozu* are about to commence the service. Now, boys, be very respectful, and do not make loud remarks about what you see."

"All right, papa," murmured Fitz. "Say, Oto, why do they have that screen of fine wire before the altar?"

"To keep people from firing spit-ball prayers at the image of Buddha," answered Oto, in his usual tone. "You need not lower your voices until the service begins."

The main altar was enclosed with a rail, the space thus shut off occupying about one third of the temple. On each side of the sanctuary were square posts, lacquered black, upon which sacred sentences were inscribed in letters of gold, and behind the pillars were enormous lanterns of silk, covered with texts.

Right and left of the screen were triple frames filled with candles, that twinkled like rows of stars. Between the candle-stands was an upright post, surmounted by a slab, on which rested a bronze urn that sent forth clouds of incense.

The boys noted all this, and the motionless *bozu*, who sat behind two metal bowls on the right of the altar; also a number of tablets placed upon a side-altar on the left of the main one, which articles Oto said were spirit-tablets, bearing the posthumous names of deceased members of the congregation.

The pungent smoke of the incense permeated the building,

BUDDHIST BOZU (MINISTERS) AT PRAYER.

and made the eyes of the strangers smart. It had a peculiar odor, and Fitz remarked, —

"I believe they have put cayenne pepper in that stuff."

After a while worshippers began to arrive, and soon the temple was tolerably crowded with men, women, and children.

The festival was to commemorate the death of one of Buddha's disciples, and the *bozu* had decorated the high altar with artificial lotus-flowers, made of silk and paper.

As the people entered they fell upon their hands and knees, and bowing their heads to the mats, murmured, —

"*Namu, Amida, Butsu!*" (Hail, omnipotent Buddha!)

Then the women repeated a rosary and counted their beads, and the men sat up on their heels and smoked their tiny-bowled pipes.

About eight o'clock a *bozu* began to strike a big bell, hung in a low pagoda in the temple-grounds.

"Now for the fun," said Fitz.

"Hush!" signalled his father. "Remember this is a Japanese church."

When the vibrations of the bell had died away, four *bozu* entered the porch, and facing the people placed their hands palm to palm, and intoned in a low, sing-song, —

"*Na-a-a-mu! A-a-a—mi-i-da! B-u-u-uts!*"

They were all shaven-headed, and three of them were mere boys. Repeating their chant nine times, they slipped off their foot-gear and filed into a curtained recess on the left of the sanctuary.

Soon the veil was raised, and a procession came forth, bells were rung, the *bozu*, on the right of the altar, struck the metal bowls, and the chief *bozu*, clad in gorgeous vestments, advanced into the railed enclosure, behind him being an incense-bearer, who wore a strange cap. After them defiled a number of sub-*bozu*, clothed in colored robes.

A tedious ceremonial followed; bells were rung, incense burnt, and more candles lighted, while the *bozu* chanted, in solemn chorus, the one prayer, —

"*Namu, Amida, Butsu!*"

Every now and again the worshippers would join loudly

in the prayer, then fill and light their pipes as though they were in a theatre.

During the service a lay-brother went silently round the

SERVICE IN THE BUDDHIST TEMPLE.

altar-rails and peddled holy candles, his customers waiting for his approach with clasped hands and bowed heads.

After the officiating *bozu* had retired, the four who had

first entered reappeared, carrying low tables, on which piles of narrow slips of paper were neatly arranged. They marched into the enclosure, bowed before the altar, seated themselves near the rails, and placed the trays before them.

Each was provided with a portable writing-apparatus, containing brushes, and a sponge moistened with ink.

Their appearance caused quite a commotion among the worshippers, who crowded about the new-comers, shouting,—

"Ten prayers for me!"

"Five for me!"

"One for me, for good luck at fishing!"

"One for me, that I may find a pot of money!"

The *bozu* listened unmoved until the crowd formed into lines, when they attended to each person in turn.

Some wanted prayers that were ready printed, others requested special ones to be written for them, the price of the latter varying with the length of the petition.

As the purchasers received the strips, they put them in their mouths and chewed them to pulp; then advancing to the centre of the altar-rail, threw the pellets at the wire screen before the image of Buddha.

"What do you think of all this, Sallie?" inquired Oto of the amazed girl.

"I think it is dreadfully silly," she whispered. "You don't believe in it, do you, Oto?"

"No," he answered; "it is very shocking to see my countrymen thus steeped in ignorance."

"Look at that old woman," said Fitz, with a chuckle; "she has had three shots, and missed every time. Jeminy!"

"Come," said Mrs. Jewett, "suppose we return to the inn; I have seen enough of this."

They sent a boy round to the front entrance to procure their shoes, then quitted the temple by a rear porch, in which was suspended an enormous painting, representing the trial of sinners by Ema, the god of the nether regions, who, though he had a back seat in the picture, was depicted five times as large as any of the sinners occupying the foreground. These unfortunates were regarding their future fate in a metal mirror held by a horned demon.

PICTURE OF BUDDHIST LAST JUDGMENT.

As the visitors quitted the grounds, the Professor said, —

"I am both shocked and amazed, — shocked to see a portion of an otherwise intelligent people so steeped in superstition; and amazed to notice how happy and light-hearted they all appear."

"Yes," said Mrs. Jewett; "I did not see a sad face among

them. They seemed to look upon the service as a duty to be performed as soon as possible."

"I think the spit-ball prayers were comical," said Fitz. "I'd like to have had a shot or two, so I would!"

"Oh, brother," whispered Sallie; "you forget that is idolatry."

"Yes," he answered; "still, I think it is fun all the same."

Upon arriving at the inn, they found the place in great confusion.

"Oh!" cried one of the waitresses. "Our master is dying!"

## CHAPTER IV.

### NAGASAKI BY NIGHT.

"When evening spreads her veil over the city,
Go forth and watch the scenes in the houses:
It is thus you will learn the ways of the people."
JAPANESE POEM.

OTO quieted the girls by informing them that he was a medical student, then went to the host's apartment, where he found the sufferer in the hands of two quacks. One of them, an old fellow, who wore spectacles, was feeling the patient's pulse, and the other was holding the man in a sitting position. On the matted floor were a medicine-chest, and a bundle containing a box of herbs.

As Oto entered the room their hostess, bearing a tub of hot liquid, advanced to her husband, and said, —

"Here is the infusion of oak-leaves."

"One moment, honorable wife," sternly remarked the elder of the quacks; "I find the *yo* (hot) principle predominates in your husband's body; we must therefore give him *in* (cold) infusions."

"Shall I open the medicine-chest?" inquired his assistant.

"Yes," nodded the senior partner. "Honorable wife, come and support your husband while we prescribe for him."

The woman, who was greatly agitated, obeyed, and the younger practitioner proceeded to unfasten the packages.

"Give him a dose of deer-horn powder, with a pinch of dried toad-dust," continued the old quack, who was still examining the patient's pulse. "This is a severe case of fever in the bones, and requires to be treated with a powerful remedy."

Hearing this, Oto lost patience, and, advancing, exclaimed: "You impostors! You talk like Chinese doctors. Get out of this, and leave the man to me; I will cure him in twenty-four hours!"

Thus speaking, he drove the quacks out of the room, and, addressing the amazed landlady, said, —

THE SICK LANDLORD AND THE QUACKS.

"Do not be alarmed; I am a graduate of the Imperial College of Tokio, and have studied medicine abroad. Now let me examine your husband. Deer-horn powder and dried toad-dust indeed! Such rubbish would only make the sick man worse."

He proceeded to ascertain the sufferer's malady, — after doing which, he said, —

"This is a case of intermittent fever. I will prepare you some medicine that will relieve him. Do not let those quacks see him again, or I will not answer for the consequences."

He gave her minute instructions how to nurse her husband, and told her he would visit him every hour, then returned to his friends.

"Well," asked Johnnie; "is the man dead?"

"No," quietly answered Oto. "He soon would have been if I had not gone to his rescue. Those quacks kill five persons where they cure one."

"So do ours at home," said Mrs. Jewett. "Are there no regular practitioners in Japan?"

"Yes," returned Oto. "Our government has built hospitals in every city, and is doing everything in its power to expose the wretches who prey on the credulity of our people; still, I think ignorant folks rather like being quacked," adding, with a smile, "I found it so in the States!"

"We, as a nation, believe in humbug," said the Professor. "Although we have the very best surgeons and physicians in the world, many of our citizens prefer to consult impostors, and to swallow patent medicines. You Japanese are no worse than we are."

"Thank you, Professor," said Oto, bowing. "Come, are you ready for dinner?"

They all answered in the affirmative, and their friend went to the kitchen to order the meal.

After a brief delay, a number of servants entered, bearing *zen* (low tables) filled with dishes of food, which they set before each of the party. When the covers were removed the attendants retired, and, the Professor having asked a blessing, Oto said, —

"You will find this bean-soup nice; the lumps in it are pieces of fish. That clear white food is raw carp; it is very good. The boiled fish is also excellent. The vegetables are potatoes, turnips, and mushrooms."

"Raw fish!" murmured Johnnie. "Who ever heard of eating fish in that style?"

"Try it before you condemn it," said Oto. "You eat lots of raw fish in the States."

"We do?" cried Fitz, who was ruefully regarding his food. "Bet you we never do."

"Fitz," gently remarked his mother, "you must not say 'bet,'— it is vulgar."

"Well, we don't eat raw fish, anyhow," growled the lad. "Where are the knives and forks?"

"You must eat with chopsticks," said his father, taking two from a bowl. "Remember, you agreed to live in Japanese fashion, and must give it a thorough trial. Oto, you say we eat raw fish in America, — what do you mean? I never indulged in such a —— luxury."

"Never ate oysters on the half-shell, or Little-Neck clams, sir?" slyly inquired Oto.

"You have me there," laughingly answered the Professor. "Come, wife, come, Sallie, and you, my sons, give Japanese food a trial."

A great number of little dishes, containing relishes, were on each table; and after Oto had told them the nature of these condiments, they began to eat.

"This *shoyu* is nice," said Fitz, referring to a sort of catsup. "Say, Oto, where is the meat?"

"You will not find any in a regular Japanese hotel," he answered. "If you want that sort of thing you must go to a shop where they sell foreign food."

"Oh!" muttered Fitz; "this *is* a country."

Oto's eyes twinkled, and he merrily retorted, —

"That's just what I said of America when I first landed!"

They contrived to make a good meal, though none but the Professor and Oto touched the uncooked food.

"We have not been educated to that," remarked Mrs. Jewett. "It may be nice, still I have no desire to try it."

The afternoon was spent in writing home and in resting, the weather being very sultry.

After supper, they sallied out to see Nagasaki by night.

The living-rooms were all open to the street, and the occupations and amusements of the inhabitants could be seen with-

THE GAME OF CATCHING THE FOX.

out the spectator entering the dwellings. Upon the party halting before a house in which some men and women were shouting, laughing, and enjoying themselves, Mrs. Jewett motioned her husband to go on, when Oto said,—

"You need have no scruples; it does not hurt the people to look at them. Those folks are playing a game called 'Catch the Fox.'"

The head of the family noticed the strangers, and invited them into the veranda, then begging them to excuse him, resumed his sport, he acting the part of the fox.

It was a strange scene. The lamps threw dark shadows, and but partly lighted the apartment, where nine persons were collected, — six of the party being men, and the remainder women. Two males, stripped to the waist, sat nearest the balcony, holding a rope, in the centre of which was an open noose. Behind the latter was a *sambo* (stand), supporting a small bowl filled with *saké* (rice wine).

Two of the women began to play *samisen* (guitars), while the men on their left beat time with sticks, which they struck on cups or clashed together.

The host, who wore nothing but his trousers, tied a fan on the top of his head, which caused his shadow to resemble that of a fox, hence the name of the sport. He danced, jumped, and gambolled like a schoolboy, artfully advancing backwards and sideways until close to the noose, when he would suddenly drop upon the ground, and, inserting his head, endeavor to touch the bowl. If he succeeded, he was permitted to drink the contents; but whenever he failed, the watchers tightened the noose and captured him, and everybody yelled with delight.

It was a rough, coarse amusement; still, they all appeared to enjoy it, and there was no dissent or quarrelling.

The Jewetts quitted the scene, and walked on until they came to a perambulating astronomer, who was loudly calling attention to his telescope, — with which, he assured the spectators, he could see "the hares scouring the face of the moon with rushes!"

In one hand he held a blazing torch of bruised bamboo, and in the other a powerful magnifying-glass.

After a while a coolie advanced, and paying him a few cash, said, —

"I want to see the hares at work."

"Close one eye, and apply the other to the telescope," said the crafty fellow; "you will then behold the lovely animals."

The coolie did as he was directed, gaping all the while in a puzzled fashion; then he said, —

"I can't see the hares."

"Oh, they are there," gravely answered the exhibitor. "Pay for another peep, and try again."

The greenhorn handed over a second fee, and renewed his gaze, presently remarking, —

A PERIPATETIC ASTRONOMER.

"I think I see their tails!"

"Yes," was the sly response; "they have just retired into their holes! Now, don't gape any more at them; these foreign gentlemen desire to see the wonderful sight."

He pushed the coolie away, and cried, —

"Oh — yes — this is a splendid instrument; everybody of importance looks through it," — adding, with a sly grimace at the crowd: "It once belonged to the Emperor of America!"

When the Professor endeavored to direct the telescope toward the evening star, he found the works would not move; and noticing his attempt, the astronomer said, —

"My lord, please don't interfere with it. It is not lucky to spy at anything but the moon."

Johnnie told him that the planet was not inhabited by hares, but the fellow only grinned, and said, —

SHADOWS ON THE WALL.

"All right; you say it is not, I say it is! Now, as neither you nor I have ever been there, who is to tell which of us is right?"

They left him, and he resumed his cry, —

"Honorable masters, come and see the hares at work polishing the moon!"

Oto conducted his party into the main street, and said, —

"Our ignorant folks think those spots on the face of the moon are hares cleaning the surface of the planet with *equisetum* (scouring rushes). Is it not ridiculous?"

"It is not more absurd than our ancestors' belief that there was a man in the moon," answered Mrs. Jewett.

"I think the showman was smart," said Fitz. "He scarcely gave the coolie time to peep before he asked for a second fee. He beats the telescope man on Boston Common."

In one house they beheld a woman making shadow-pictures on the screens, to amuse her two elder children; while her third, an infant, calmly slept upon the floor of the apartment.

She produced many clever results by using her fingers and the drapery of her dress,— one shadow, that of a fox on its hind legs, being very clearly represented.

PLAYING CARDS.

On seeing the strangers, she squatted upon the floor, and her children ran to her, crying,—

"*Mogu!*" (Chinese.)

"Come," said Mrs. Jewett, "we will not intrude any longer."

They halted a little further down the street in order to watch a family playing cards. There were four men and two women, and all of them talked at once; shouting and laughing as though they were having a good time.

The cards were inscribed with halves of verses, and the game was to secure as many complete sets as possible. First, the dealer gave each person six cards from his pack; then the player on his left shouted, —

"The beautiful lotus springs from the mud."

"*Hai* (yes); hand it this way!" cried one of the women, exhibiting a card bearing the other half of the verse, viz., —

"Thus the soul of man emerges from its sin!"

"Very poetic," murmured the Professor.

"Yes," said Fitz; "but I prefer cribbage. That game of theirs is like our 'Authors.'"

They left them matching verses, and laughing as though it were immense fun.

After walking some distance, they entered a tea-house, where the people were listening to a celebrated singer who had recently arrived from Tokio. She knelt behind a low music-stand, and played a *samisen* (guitar), using an ivory instrument to touch the strings. A dead silence prevailed among the audience, and as soon as the foreigners were supplied with tea, the singer began, —

"*Yagai sosho asei kamabe-sushi!*" (When the frogs sing noisily in the fields.)

This was shrieked in a quavering falsetto, that caused the ladies to wince, the Professor to close his eyes, and the boys to chuckle.

The singer twanged her instrument, shook her notes, hung on one of the latter for half a minute at a time, and, following the Japanese idea, set at defiance every canon of our musical art; winding up with a sudden gasp, as though something had broken in her lungs.

Oto, who had listened with breathless admiration, turned to Fitz and whispered, —

"What do you think of *that?*"

"She's almost killed mother!" replied the young monkey. "I feel melancholy! Let us get out of this."

To their surprise, the Professor decided to remain. He said the music interested him, and that it resembled Wagner's.

A FAMOUS SINGER.

However, when he saw his wife's appealing look, he rose and led the way out.

"Oto," remarked Mrs. Jewett, on reaching the now deserted street, "please never take me to hear a singer again: another such treat would completely shatter my nerves."

"Why, didn't you like it?" asked Oto. "I thought you were fond of music."

"That is not music at all,—it's pandemonium!" said Johnnie. "Oh, my! didn't she squall?"

"I am very sorry," answered Oto. "O-Den is considered one of our best singers; I thought her voice very charming."

NIGHT WATCHMEN.

"Oto," said Sallie, "now I know why you did not admire Miss Kellogg. I understand—there is a wide gulf between Japanese and American music."

"A sea—not a gulf, but a whole ocean!" murmured Fitz. "Hello! what is that jingling noise?"

They looked in front of them and beheld three men advancing with staves, on which were iron rings that jingled as the bearers struck the poles upon the cobble-stones. Each of the new-comers also carried a long lantern, and shouted, in a querulous voice,—

"*Hi-no Yojin!*" (Look out for fire.)

"These are private watchmen," said Oto; "they still keep them on here. In Tokio they have uniformed policemen who do that sort of duty."

"What duty?" queried Johnnie.

"Why, cry the hour, and scare off the thieves. They march at certain hours all over the city. The robbers, who always know when the watchmen are coming, hide until the patrol has passed."

"That is what our burglars do," said Fitz. "After all, some Japanese things are very much like American."

"Not the music," laughingly observed Sallie.

"My dear," gravely remarked her father, "you ridicule Japanese music because you cannot understand it. Wait until you have heard more of the melodies. There is something very weird and melancholy in their airs."

"Very melancholy!" said his wife. "Come, Professor, it is time these young people were in bed. I like Japan, and have been much entertained by what I have seen this evening; still, I do not believe I shall ever learn to admire the music of the country."

They returned to their hotel, where they found a night-porter waiting up for them.

"How is your master?" inquired Oto.

The man averted his face, as a Japanese does when he desires to say something he deems will be unpleasant, and muttered, —

"Oh! they're at him again!"

"Who?" queried Oto.

"Those quacks," was the cautious reply. "As soon as you quitted the house, my honorable mistress admitted them."

Oto, who was very indignant at this, went straight to the landlord's room, and, throwing open the screen, beheld a sight that made his blood boil.

The host, muttering deliriously, was kneeling near a lamp, while the spectacled doctor was placing small patches of vegetable fibre, at regular intervals, on each side of his patient's spine.

He had just succeeded in affixing the eighth patch, and was about to fire them with a taper he held in his left hand, when

APPLYING THE MOXA.

Oto rushed forward, and removing the moxa, ordered the fellow to be gone.

An animated wrangle ensued, during which the Professor and the boys appeared on the scene.

"What is the trouble?" demanded the gentleman, glancing at the old doctor, who scowled at Oto. "Is the patient worse?"

"He soon would have been," replied the young man. "I arrived just in time to save him." Then, turning to the quack, he cried: "Get out of this! or I'll burn a moxa on you."

As the doctor beat a hurried retreat, Fitz, who had merrily regarded the scene, inquired, —

"What is a moxa, — a fire-cracker?"

"No; it is the fibrous leaf of a mountain plant, rubbed into a sort of tinder, and used in pellets on the skin. These lumps are fired, and often burn deeply into the flesh. It is all very well in some cases, but useless in this."

When Oto had seen the sick man back to bed, he said to the landlady, —

"Why did you admit that quack? You know I gave you strict orders not to do so."

"Honorable doctor," murmured the agitated hostess, "it was not my fault. His mother came here and ordered me to send for Doctor Bonsan again. What can a woman do when her mother-in-law says nay?"

They all laughed, and Oto bade her good-night, remarking, —

"I'll see the old lady to-morrow.

## CHAPTER V.

#### KILLING TIME AT AN INN.

The rain descends like the fall of Kiri-furi
I am weary of staying in doors.
When we travel we must expect to be miserable;
Still the landlord and his wife
Make our prison as pleasant as possible.
Let us therefore be contented with
The liquid gift of the Gods. — JAPANESE POEM.

THE month of July proved a very wet one, and the travellers had plenty of time to study life in a Japanese inn.

Their landlord, who had quite recovered, was most kind. He showed them rolls of pictures (*makimono*), and sat with them for hours, describing the scenes and amusing his guests with his witty comments.

One day he brought a *kakemono* (hanging picture), and squatting on the floor, said, —

"This is a very old painting by my grandfather. It represents the twelve great signs."

The boys moved near to him, and he unrolled the picture, which was beautifully executed in gold and colors.

"Are not those your signs for the months of the year and the hours of the day?" inquired Fitz, pointing to the figures. "Please explain them to us."

"You are correct in your surmise," replied the man. "We, like the Chinese, divide our day into twelve hours, which we named after these signs. Now, we are beginning to use the foreign terms for the hours. This sign of the rat means the hour from midnight until two in the morning. The next sign,

THE GOLDEN RIVER.

A PICNIC.

# KILLING TIME AT AN INN. 65

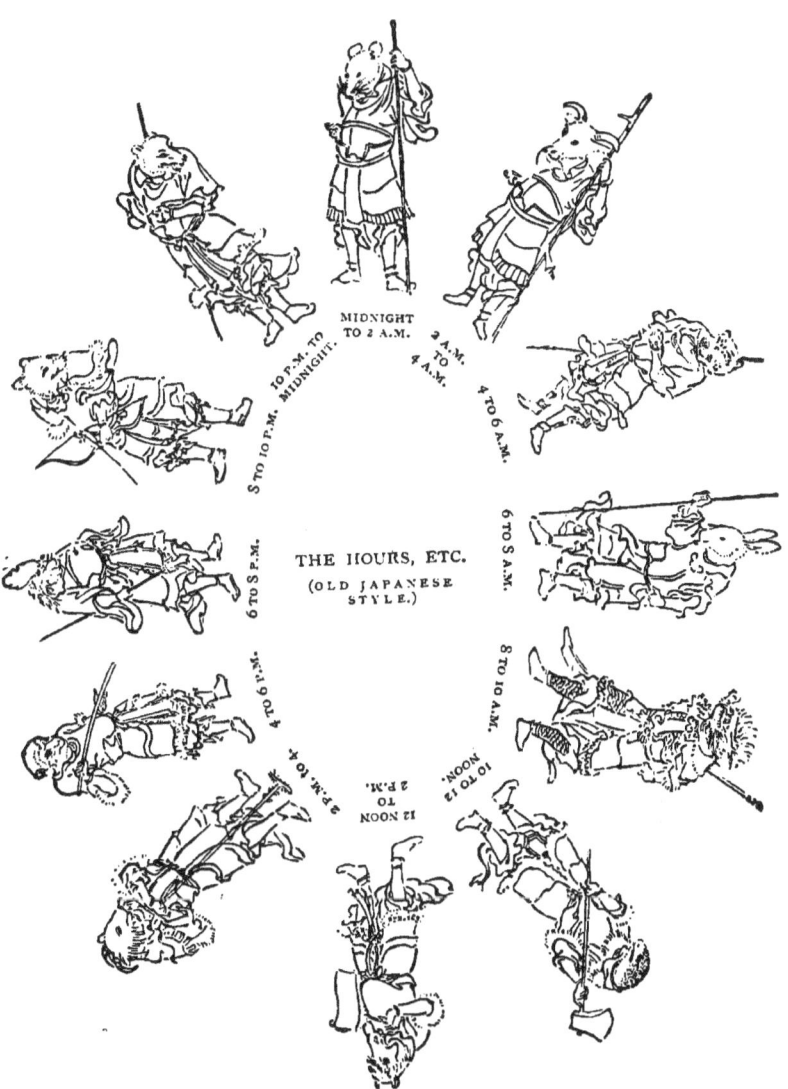

THE JAPANESE SIGNS FOR THE HOURS.

the ox, denotes the hour from two to four. Then come the tiger, the hare, the dragon and snake,— the last signifying from ten to twelve o'clock of your time. After that follow the horse, the ram, the ape, the rooster, the hog and the fox."

"Those were long hours," said Sallie.

"Yes," he replied. "Particularly when one was sick."

"You formerly called some years after those signs, did you not?" asked Johnnie.

"Yes," said Oto. "We thus named periods, years and months. Now we divide our year as you do and date from the first one of the Mikado's reign. This is the seventh month, thirteenth year of the Emperor's rule."

When they had discussed the merits of the picture, their host retired and presently returned with a number of scrolls, which he unrolled and exhibited with evident pride.

HERONS AND SMALL BIRDS.

"This," he said, "is a painting of our birds after Hokusai. It was done by my brother."

"Who was Hokusai?" asked Fitz.

"He was one of our greatest artists," replied their host. "He designed the *Manguwa* (ten thousand sketches), and originated this style of spirited drawing in outline."

"I have read about him in Professor Morse's writings," remarked Johnnie.

"Morse?" said the landlord, smiling. "You mean the good friend to Japan who taught in the Imperial College at Tokio. My son studied under him. *Hai-hai!* he knows all about Hokusai. His pupils remember him with affectionate regard, he is a great scholar."

After they had examined the picture of the herons and doves, he showed them a sketch of a badger climbing a bamboo.

"That is what we term a silhouette," said Mrs. Jewett. "It is very good."

"Yes," said the landlord. "It was done by my brother. Here is another picture after Hokusai, *gan* (geese) fishing, a king-fisher, and some swallows. That large bird is a stork, the emblem of long life."

"Have you any picture by Hokusai?" asked the Professor.

The man carefully re-rolled his treasures and, bowing, retired. In a few moments he returned with a *makemono* which he untied, saying,—

"This was done by a pupil of the great artist, and is a copy of a celebrated picture. It represents blind men,— shampooers,— crossing a river."

BADGER ON A BAMBOO.

"What funny faces they have," cried Fitz.

"Yours would be just as comical were you sightless," gently answered their host. "See, they are depicted feeling their way with their staves, and some are holding on by the belt of the person before them."

"It is a wonderfully life-like picture," remarked the Professor. "Do you know my brother, Dr. Jewett."

"My son does," was the response. "I have never had the pleasure of having a limb removed by your honorable relative."

This speech caused the travellers to smile, when the landeord said,—

"Indeed, they tell me he does it like blinking one's eyes. Ah! you Americans are a wonderful people. Would you like to hear a lady perform on the *koto* (harp)? I have a guest who will be pleased to play for your entertainment."

"Does she sing?" inquired Mrs. Jewett.

GEESE, SWALLOWS, AND KING-FISHER.

MEKURA HININ, BEGGARS BLIND.

"Unfortunately, no," answered the man.

All said they would be charmed to hear her perform on the national instrument, hearing which the landlord retired, and, after a brief delay, returned with a young girl, who was followed by a servant bearing a curious apparatus which he deposited on the floor.

The performer bowed gracefully, then, fitting some ivory

PLAYING THE KOTO (HARP).

tips on her fingers, began to tune the instrument, one end of which was supported by two legs while the other rested on the mats.

She moved the bridges and touched each string sharply, then began to play a bewildering air. Sometimes the Jewetts imagined she was about to execute a tune, and listened to catch it, but in another moment she struck an inharmonious note, and to their disappointment ended the melody. After playing several times, she bowed, received their thanks and retired.

"Your music is like your singing," said Mrs. Jewett. "Just as one thinks one can make out a connected tune, off goes the air at a tangent, and, oh dear! it is not what we call harmony."

"Come," said Oto. "The rain has ceased, let us go to the drug-store. I want to buy some medicine for a child belonging to one of the guests. My patient is a pretty little fellow who wears his hair in the American fashion."

MASTER SHIUICHIRO AND HIS NURSE.

"I would so like to see him," said Sallie.

"He has gone for an airing, though I think he will be back in a moment," said Oto. "I wish to tell his nurse something before we go out. The poor child has lost his mother, and were it not for his attendant, would fare badly, as his father is employed in the custom-house, and is away all day."

Presently they glanced out of the window and saw a girl coming along the street, carrying a little boy on her back.

"That is Master Shiuichiro," said Oto. "Is he not a dear fellow? His nurse, O-Momo, takes him everywhere. See, she has stopped, and is telling him to wave his hand to me."

Johnnie sketched the pair, and when the girl entered with her charge, showed her the picture.

She had, of course, left her clogs in the veranda, so did not look quite as tall as when on the street.

Shiuichiro was naturally very shy; however he quickly took a liking to Sallie, who invited the nurse to bring him to their room some evening.

"All aboard for a walk," shouted Fitz. "After being kept a prisoner by the rain, I'm just hungry for a run in the fresh air. Come, Sallie, kiss the child and hurry up. I want to make an important purchase."

When the girl attempted to do as her brother suggested, Shiuichiro resisted, saying, —

"No, no! I don't like it. You hurt me."

"He does not understand kissing," quietly observed Oto. "When we salute a child affectionately, we rub him on the top of his head."

"Did you never kiss your mother?" asked Mrs. Jewett.

"Never," he replied. "If I were to do such a thing, my honorable mother would imagine I had taken leave of my senses."

"And yet you love her, Oto?"

"Yes, ma'am. I do not think any one would doubt that. I have written to my honorable mother every week since I left her; and since I have arrived here have sent her a letter every day. She is the first in my heart."

They quitted the inn, and walked toward the pharmacy; Oto going first with Johnnie, and Fitz taking care of Sallie.

The people were very civil, and nobody molested them; though the Professor's long hair and broad-brimmed hat were the subjects of much subdued comment on the part of the children, who evidently took him for a lady.

"What is yonder man doing with that magnifying-glass?"

asked Johnnie, pointing to a group of persons in front of a little restaurant, the entrance of which was garnished with birds and vegetables, and bore the following sign: —

*The Most Nourishing Foreign Food
Always on hand by
Yomo Yasunosuke.*

"He is a palmister," replied Oto; "and is endeavoring to induce that shampooer to have his fortune told. Let us watch them. Those fellows are most amusing impostors."

The man was squatting near the right of the entrance, before him being spread a cloth on which were some books, writing-materials, and two magnifying-glasses.

On his right was a blind man, neatly clad, who, as he squatted, rested his pole on his shoulder, and held his rain umbrella in his hand.

On a bench to their left sat a peddler, who leaned upon his pack and watched the speaker; as also did two ruddy-faced waitresses, who evidently took a great interest in the proceedings.

Oto motioned his friends to hurry forward, and the party halted and listened.

The palmister wore a towel on his head, and had an immense mouth, the corners of which he from time to time slily twitched.

"Yes, yes!" he cried, holding one of the magnifying-glasses in his left hand, and examining the fingers of his right. "I am the man who can tell your fortune, Mr. Swampmeadow. Come, do not be so stingy. I will reveal your future for ten *sen* (cents). Let me look at the palm of your right hand, and I will predict just what sort of luck you are going to have and how long you will live."

The blind man chuckled, and sarcastically replied, —

"That is too cheap. As to my luck, I am satisfied. With

regard to how long I have to live, only the gods know that. I prefer to keep my money."

A PALMISTER AND HIS CUSTOMER.

"You rich shampooers are all as mean as possible," growled the palmister.

"What will you charge me?" inquired one of the waitresses, squatting near him and exhibiting her plump palm.

"I will tell your fortune for a bowl of rice and a cup of tea," he said. "It is a pleasure to examine such a pretty hand. Shall I reveal your future?"

"Go ahead!" she laughingly answered.

"What nonsense!" said Fitz in a loud tone. "Scsch," breathed Johnnie, "you will spoil the fun."

The palmister gravely examined the lines on her hand, then said in an oracular manner,—

"You are indeed a fortunate girl. Here is a money-line leading from the thumb to the wrist. You will marry a rich merchant and go to foreign countries. If you will give me ten *sen*, I will tell you something very good that I see on your index finger."

She produced the money from a paper kept in the bosom of her robe, and nervously handed it to him, when he critically examined the finger to which he had referred, and said,—

"You are a favorite of the gods. You will live to be over a hundred years old, and have very wealthy descendants, who will honor your memory for centuries."

"All for ten *sen!*" chuckled the blind man. "Go to—why, I would predict her marriage with an *ex-daimio* (lord) for half that sum."

Then turning his sightless eyes toward the group of foreigners, he said,—

"Want to be shampooed, your excellencies?"

"How could you tell we were present?" asked the Professor.

"I could smell the sweet perfume used by your ladies," answered the man. "I have eyes in my nose, ears and fingers."

"Come," said Johnnie, "this will never take us to the drugstore."

They left the palmister, who was endeavoring to induce the peddler to have his hands examined, and followed the main

DRUG STORE.

street until they reached a large building, the front of which was protected with wooden bars.

"It looks like a wild-beast show," said Fitz. "Why do they bar it off in that way?"

"To keep out the loafers," slily answered Oto.

"The proprietors of our country drug-stores should imitate that plan," laughingly remarked Johnnie.

The narrow sidewalk before the building was neatly flagged for the convenience of customers, who waited there while their prescriptions were being prepared. Above this projected a pent roof, heavily tiled and decorated with signs; similar notices being suspended from the front of the store.

The advertisements written were in Chinese characters, and read as follows: —

"Imperial Jinseng."
"Imperial Asafœtida."
"Complete Tranquillity Pills."

The scene was a busy one, and the friends halted to watch it.

On the left was a shaven-headed doctor of the old school, carrying in one hand a rain umbrella, which he still kept open, and holding in the other a fan.

Behind him marched his scantily-dressed servant, bearing a medicine-chest.

A little further on was a coolie, who still kept his bearing-stick on his shoulder, but who rested one of his burdens on the flags while he waited for some herbs which a salesman was mixing in a huge bowl.

"What is that long, white vegetable on the man's load, under his rain hat?" asked Sallie.

"That is a *dai-kon* (radish)," replied Oto. "It sometimes grows to an immense size. We use it to make that strongly perfumed pickle of which you complained at Golden River."

"The pickle that smelt like Limburger cheese," said Fitz. "I shall never forget its odor."

"What is that machine the coolie is carrying?" asked John. "It has horns. Is it an advertisement?"

"No, it is a child's toy, and represents an ancient helmet. You will see lots of them in Tokio during the Feast of Flags, our boys' festival."

At the next compartment, a man was buying herbs, which the shopman handed through the bars for him to examine.

"He is a poor quack," said Oto. "He has no one to carry his medicine-case."

As he was speaking, some ladies appeared with a child, who, though scarcely able to toddle, insisted on not being led.

"That is the son of an ex-lord," whispered Oto. "A few years ago he would not have been permitted to walk in the streets. Now he can enjoy himself."

A boy, on his way to the store to have a cup filled with drugs, watched the little fellow, and said, in a mocking tone,—

"*Hai!* I like to see such things. It shows that the nobles are made the same way we are."

The ladies frowned at this, but the saucy fellow only laughed, and continued,—

"Oh, we are all alike, now! We are not obliged to wait for that until we die."

The little gentleman regarded him disdainfully, then moved on followed by his mother and servants; behind them being a male attendant, who walked with his head respectfully bowed.

A young merchant, who had regarded the scene from under the shade of his fan, turned away, and, addressing Oto, said,—

"That boy is right. Still the nobles have the money and can afford to look down on us."

"Not on me," quickly returned Oto. "I am as good as any noble."

"I understand. You have been in America," said the merchant.

"Is that man carrying a pipe?" asked Sallie, pointing to a coolie bearing a curious instrument.

"No, it is an inhaler," laughingly replied Oto. "Our quacks prescribe them for all kinds of diseases. He is going to have it filled at the drug-store."

"Inhaler," said Johnnie.

"Yes, the patient places certain herbs and drugs in that bowl and inhales the air through the tube. It is a pure piece of quackery, much affected by my countrymen."

"And ours," quietly observed Professor Jewett. "Inhalation relieves some diseases, but will not cure any. Quacks are alike, all over the world."

The visitors approached the store, and when Oto had made his purchases, Johnnie asked the shopman,—

"What sort of drugs do you keep?"

"All kinds," answered the man. "Our largest trade is in pills, draughts and plasters, that are said to cure every ailment, though I never take or use them myself. When I am sick I go to a doctor who practises in the foreign style."

"You are wise," said Oto. "Come, boys, we are keeping away the customers."

They quitted the store and went toward the shore, passing many shops devoted to the sale of foreign goods.

"Ah, here is what I want," cried Fitz, indicating a knife and fork in a case. "Now I am happy. How much are those, Mr. Shopkeeper?"

"Five *yen*," calmly returned the man. "I bought the instruments as a great curiosity. People come to my store to see them."

"Five dollars for an iron knife and a two-tined, rusty, old fork," ruefully exclaimed the boy. "Jeminy! before I'll pay that,

I'll master the art of eating with *hashi* (chopsticks). Come along, he may keep his old things."

They walked on until they came to a pipe-maker's, where they saw two men engraving patterns on the stems of the tiny-bowled articles. They did not use a graver, as our artisans do, but employed sharp punches and little hammers of steel, with which they produced beautiful flowing patterns.

AN ENGRAVER OF PIPES.

The elder of the men wore round spectacles and sang as he worked, his journeyman sometimes joining in the air, which was to the foreigners of the usual distressing kind.

He kept on, never glancing up to notice the strangers, and the sound of his hammer resembled the "tap, tap, tap" of a woodpecker on a tree-trunk.

They proceeded from the pipe-maker's to the fish-market, which smelt strongly and was an inch deep in mud.

"What has that man got in those enormous buckets?" asked Sallie, glancing at a vendor of salt who was chatting with a house-servant, whose face was swathed in a towel.

Oto told her, adding, —

" Our best salt comes from Ako, on the shore of the Inland Sea. It is, however, when compared with the American article, of a bad color, and full of grit and impurities. The kind that man is selling is coarse, and only used for preserving fish and making *daikon* (pickled radish)."

A PEDDLER OF SALT.

A brief inspection of the market sufficed, and the visitors were glad to retreat toward the main avenue of the city, from whence proceeded sounds of drumming and shouting.

On turning a corner they found themselves in a place where four streets met.

To their right was a tobacconist's shop, in which sat a woman sorting the weed, while her son watched the antics of some dancers, and amused himself with a bob-tail cat. The outside screen of the store was decorated with pictures denoting the business, and bore the name and address of the proprietor; and suspended from a copper rod, driven in the corner-post of the building, was a gigantic sign — the head of the god Daruma, enveloped in tobacco leaves, this deity being a favorite with the lower orders of Japanese.

Upon noticing the presence of the foreigners, the dancing-boys uttered shrill cries, threw somersaults, and contorted themselves; as they did so, shaking their hideous red masks and waving their rooster-feather plumes to the sound of their leaders' tambour — while, to increase the din, two girls, carrying *samisen*, stationed themselves across the way, and began to thrum and sing at the top of their voices. One of the boys carried a long drum, which he from time to time beat vigorously, and all of them danced and performed acrobatic tricks.

When their leader heard the sound of the girls' voices, he struck his tambour harder than before, and began to sing a well-known song from the poem of the "Forty-seven Ronins."

> "*Aré yaré Shibitoi Oyazimeto*
> *Nuki hanaski nanno kumoria.*"
>
> "'Oh, pshaw, you obstinate old creature!'
> So saying, he swung his sword without any trouble."

Although his singing had an exceedingly depressing effect upon the American spectators, it appeared to exhilarate the youthful acrobats, who spun on one foot, drummed, and gave way to the excitement of the moment, as though really enjoying it. At the word of command, one of them bent his body in the form of an arch, while the other, mounting on his companion's stomach, stood upon his hands and elevated his feet in the air. Then the man threw down his tambour, and shouting to the boys, bade two of them climb upon his shoulders. The drummer unslung his instrument, and, retaining his head-dress, ascended the old fellow's body, presently standing erect on his shoulders, then whistled to one of his companions. Up went the blindfolded lad, and when he was

PERFORMING BOYS.

in position, the fourth youngster slowly mounted and soon stood erect — twelve feet from the ground.

When this was accomplished, the performers began to wag their masks and sing; as they did so, the man turned slowly round and round, then advanced toward the foreigners and gave a shrill cry, on which the uppermost lad dropped into the arms of the one beneath him, then turned a somerset and dropped to the ground; the others following him in rapid succession. The performance ended by the entire party revolving on their hands and feet, yelling and screaming like Indians.

It was astonishing to see how limber the old man was; he went over and over ten times in succession, and repeated the feat until both he and his pupils were completely exhausted, after which he approached the spectators and respectfully solicited a reward.

He said the young folks were his grandchildren, that their parents were dead, and that his wife and himself subsisted on the proceeds of their exhibition, adding, —

"They go to school, and are saving money to enable them to visit the United States and make their fortunes."

The boys removed their head-pieces, and the travellers saw they were healthy-looking and full of fun. One of them asked if everybody in America was rich; and another, whether Fitz and Johnnie owned watches. The American boys chatted with the performers for a while, among other things learning that they seldom used salt, and had never partaken of fresh meat; that their principal diet was rice, and their names were Choshichi, Seibeye, Kichiyemon, and Zensaburo.

The Professor gave the old fellow a gratuity, then led the way back to the hotel.

That night when Sallie retired to her room, she found two young women sleeping on the matted floor.

"Those are my cousins," said the landlady, who just then entered the apartment. "They have this evening arrived from Tokio, and I had not a vacant chamber. Both of them are very amiable and gentle. You will not object to their presence, or to their smoking, will you?"

"Oh, no;" answered the amazed girl. "I will not disturb them."

When the woman had gone, Sallie watched the sleepers, the apartment being lighted with an *andon* (square paper lantern).

The ladies were pretty, and were slumbering as peacefully

as infants. Their heads were propped on wooden pillows, on which they had placed rolls of paper to keep the dressing of their hair from spoiling the lacquer, and to render the articles more comfortable.

They slept, as many Japanese do, in their clothes, and were covered with a quilt shaped like a *kimono* (long robe), in the sleeves of which they from time to time thrust their arms.

Presently one of them awoke, saluted Sallie with a smile, lighted her pipe, and chatted as she smoked, in a very pleasant manner.

SLEEPING WOMEN.

"Will you not try a puff?" she asked.

"No, thank you," answered the young American. "In my country ladies never use tobacco."

"We all do," was the response. "I am sleepy again. Good-night."

Sallie regarded the slumberers for a few moments, then moving quietly toward them, examined their smoking apparatus, which consisted of a *tobako-bon* (wooden box containing a small pot filled with live charcoal, and a smaller one for ashes), furnished with a handle by which it could be carried

## KILLING TIME AT AN INN. 85

from room to room. It was neatly lacquered and was a good specimen of joiners' work.

The pipe, which was of silver, and elaborately chased with floral designs, rested on a tobacco-pouch of stamped paper that looked like leather. This and a piece of rag used to wipe the mouth-piece formed the outfit.

"My goodness!" murmured Sallie, as she surveyed the articles. "What strange tastes these ladies have. After all, their smoking is not very much worse than our girls chewing gum — both habits are bad enough."

SMOKING APPARATUS.

She then retired to her corner and, after saying her prayers, quickly joined her Japanese companions in the land of dreams.

## CHAPTER VI.

#### FAREWELL TO NAGASAKI.

> Up on the hillside among the cypresses
> Stands the bell-tower.
> At morn and night I hear its silvery tongue,
> It echoes the voice of the gods. — JAPANESE POEM.

ONE morning, in August, our travellers climbed the hillside and visited the great bell whose tones they had so often heard at sunrise, noon, and sunset.

"There it is!" exclaimed Fitz, as they reached the level space on which the tower was built. "My gracious! is it not a big fellow?"

The object of his remark was suspended in a frame formed of four tree-trunks, smoothed and polished, the timbers of the roof being beautifully carved and the roof itself heavily tiled.

On each side of the tower were frames to which were affixed papers, inscribed with the names and sums given by various persons to keep the structure in repair.

"I would sweep those away," said Sallie. "They disfigure the place."

"If you did no one would give anything," replied Oto. "People like to have the amount of their gifts made public, and many persons who now contribute would not do so if their names were kept secret."

"Just as our folks do when asked to give to the church building-fund," said Fitz.

BELL TOWER.

"Yes, human nature is the same everywhere," observed Mrs. Jewett.

As they approached the structure, the keeper, who was squatting and dozing in the shade on the left, rose and vanished round the corner, presently returning dressed in a *kimono* (long coat).

No Japanese is now allowed to go unclothed, and the man evidently feared he would be reported to the police. He was very civil, and led the visitors up the steps in the rear of the tower, and showed them how the bell was sounded.

"I see," said Johnnie. "You use a sort of battering-ram which you swing against the metal; it strikes and recoils, leaving the bell to vibrate. We use a clapper, which being inside the bell, checks the sound."

"There goes our ex-lord," said the keeper, pointing to a Japanese who had passed them as they approached the structure. "Ah! he formerly used to keep this place in beautiful repair, now he is poor, and all the beggars and shampooers in the city can have their names in the place of honor."

The party waited until noon, when the man drew back the beam and struck the bell, which sent forth a deafening volume of sound.

"That will do," said Mrs. Jewett. "Come away before he strikes it again. Japanese bells, like ours, sound best at a distance."

The man allowed them to get out of sight, when he again struck the bell, repeating the stroke several times at regular intervals.

After inspecting a temple near by, the party returned to the inn, where they found some students from the government college who desired an interview with the Professor. They were bright lads, and all of them spoke English.

"We wish to ask if you will honor us by delivering a

lecture on chemistry," said the spokesman. "We have plenty of apparatus and an excellent lecture-room."

That evening the Jewetts and Oto went to the college, where they were received by the Faculty, who were dressed in foreign costume.

The students, over four hundred in number, were quiet and respectful, and the Professor found everything he wanted to illustrate his discourse.

It was a wonderful sight to see the rows of earnest-looking Japanese, listening with rapt eagerness to an alien, speaking in a foreign tongue, and showing by their murmured applause that they perfectly understood every word he uttered.

When the lecture was over the Faculty warmly thanked the Professor for his kindness, and each student was presented to him.

The President then showed the gentlemen of the party through the college, which was beautifully kept and furnished in foreign style.

In the dining-hall was a painting representing the great warrior Hideyoshi or, as he is called by foreigners and illiterate people, Taiko-Sama.

"Why do you have that in an institution dedicated to the peaceful arts and sciences?" inquired Professor Jewett. "I thought Hideyoshi was a great warrior."

The President bowed, and said,—

"Hideyoshi was once a groom, but, by dint of working and studying hard, and through his natural ability, rose to be one of our greatest generals and statesmen. He founded the old college that stood on the site of this building, and was a great reformer."

"Johnnie," said the Professor, turning to his son, "you have heard of Hideyoshi. He was the General Grant of Japan."

"I thought he was a fillibuster who sent an army of invasion to the Corea," replied the boy.

"He built the *Mimidzuka* (ear-monument), at Kioto, over the ears of thousands of Coreans," said Fitz. "You know, Oto, you told me all about it."

"We are not proud of those achievements of his," said the President. "What we remember is the political reforms made by him, and the works of peace he bequeathed to us. He began what Iyeyasu perfected and ended, and he made the name of Japan respected beyond the seas."

HIDEYOSHI, LIKEWISE CALLED TAIKO-SAMA.

The gentlemen rejoined the ladies, whom they found enjoying tea and cakes.

As they returned to the inn, Fitz said,—

"I know why they put the picture of Hideyoshi in that hall."

"Why?" asked Oto.

"Because he was a smart man and was successful, like General Grant; I remember reading about him. When Japan was divided into many petty provinces, or *ken* as you term them, he whipped the chiefs or lords, and made them acknowledge the Mikado. While doing this he had an eye to his own advancement."

"Anyhow he was a great man, even though he did build a pyramid with the ears of the Coreans," said Oto. "We revere his memory just as you will that of General Grant."

"We do not revere anything," said Johnnie. "General Grant will occupy his place in our national history; but we shall never make a god of him."

"Hideyoshi is not one of our gods," warmly answered Oto.

"Come, boys," cried the Professor, from the next room. "It is time you went to sleep. Let Hideyoshi rest for to-night."

Early the next morning, Oto was called by his friend Ichiro, who said, —

"Our friend Senda is dead. You knew him well, so I hope you will go with me to condole with his family."

The young man rose, and after dressing himself in Japanese costume, wrote a letter of sympathy, then set out for the late residence of the deceased.

They found the main entrance closed with a screen of green bamboo on which was a placard, marked, —

"Peacefully reclining Spirit."

The place was surrounded by beggars, who crowded about one of the dead man's relatives and clamored for alms.

"Give me a *tempo* — give me a *tempo*," they cried. "As you are charitable, so will the gods aid your late employer."

One fellow, who wore a piece of grass-matting as a garment, yelled so loudly and was so persistent that a servant-girl, who was watching the scene, said in a low tone, —

"Give that wretch a coin, and send him away. He ought to be ashamed of himself; he is disturbing the honorable corpse."

Oto and Ichiro were admitted to the house by a side-door, and conducted to the presence of the mourners.

Near the entrance to the apartment in which the deceased was lying, were the widow and her daughter, prostrate with their faces bowed in their sleeves. The servant, who escorted the boys and a third visitor, knelt near the ladies, and quietly announced their names; the callers also kneeling, and Oto placing his letter on the mat before them.

GIVING ALMS FOR THE BENEFIT OF THE DEAD.

Then the three bowed their heads to the floor nine times, and murmured their sympathy.

The widow raised her head, and resting her face on her right hand, sobbed her thanks; after which, once more giving way to her grief, she buried her features in her sleeves and moaned pitifully.

The three young men entered the next room and glanced at their late friend, each burning a stick of incense and lighting a candle. These were placed with many others in a boat-shaped holder.

On the following day Oto, Ichiro, the Professor and his sons, attended the funeral services, which were performed in the little chapel of a cemetery situated on the outskirts of the city.

A VISIT OF CONDOLENCE.

On their way they saw the farmers cutting rice; the instruments used being of a peculiar shape — a straight blade set at right-angles to a handle.

Oto, who appeared to know everything, thus described the harvesting of rice:

"The crop is made into small bundles, and stacked in large heaps. When all the field is reaped, the laborers take the bundles separately from the stacks and cut off the heads of grain, restacking the straw neatly.

"The rice is then put in grass baskets, and carried to the threshers, who lay it on mats and beat it with flails. After this it is sieved, cleaned of its husks and packed in closely-woven, barrel-shaped grass bags, which are bound with straw ropes and carried into the barn, where they remain until the rice is used or sold."

REAPING THE RICE CROP.

When the Professor and his companions neared the cemetery, Oto said, —

"My late friend was a *samurai* (gentleman or esquire). You will see his sons dressed in our old costume. I hope the service in the chapel will not tire you."

"It cannot be more tedious than some ministers make our funeral exercises," answered Fitz. "Why, when old Mrs. Kenny was buried, they had seven clergymen to perform the service at the house, and it was so late before they got through, the family were obliged to postpone taking her to the cemetery until the next day."

REAPING THE RICE CROP.

"That will do, my son," said his father. "Here we are at the temple."

A *bozu* met them in the porch, and they were conducted into the building — a mere shed open at the sides, furnished with a large curtain and floored with pine boards.

At the far end was a screened recess, in which knelt the eldest son and three brothers of the deceased. These gentlemen wore white robes — the old mourning garb of the *samurai*.

CUTTING RICE.

The garments, having hempen wings, looked very odd to the the American boys.

In the centre of the aisle was a long table, on which stood an upright tablet inscribed with the posthumous name of the deceased, and a bronze vase filled with flowers.

On the left of this, resting on boards and trestles, was a square case covered with a white cloth, surmounted with a sort of dome bearing the *mon* (crest) of the dead gentleman.

At each corner of the case was a bamboo vase filled with evergreens.

On the right of the aisle were six Buddhist *bozu*, three of whom clanged bronze cymbals, while a fourth struck a metal bowl placed on a stand. The other two counted their beads and led the oft-repeated prayer, —

"*Namu Amida Butsu.*"

The audience was quiet and respectful; though every now and again one of the mourners would sit up, light his pipe, take a whiff, and resume his sorrowful posture.

"Where is the coffin?" whispered Fitz.

BUDDHIST FUNERAL SERVICE.

"That is it," replied Oto, pointing to the square, white box.

"That?" murmured the boy. "Is he doubled up?"

"Yes, we sometimes bury our dead with their chins resting on their knees," answered Oto.

"How uncomfortable for them," breathed Fitz. "Well, you sleep and sit differently to what we do, so I don't think it matters how you are fixed for burial."

"Hush," said his father. "Be more respectful."

The *bozu* lighted a candle for each year the deceased had lived, burnt incense and sprinkled the coffin with holy water; then after many times repeating their prayer, clashed their cymbals violently, after which the body was taken outside, and conveyed to a spot shut off with a tall screen of canvas.

The mourners and spectators followed, and saw the bearers remove the dome and cloth, and place the coffin on a pile of wood heaped under a shed.

The relatives advanced and began to count their beads and pray; three *bozu* taking their places on the opposite side of the shed and leading the exercises.

In front of the *bozu* was a table on which stood a lighted candle and three bowls containing, respectively, rice, saké and salt.

Night had closed on the scene ere the box was deposited on the pile, and the spectators could scarcely see each other's faces.

At a signal from the chief *bozu* the sexton advanced and applied the candle to the pile which had been saturated with spirits of wine. It flashed and flickered, revealing the faces of the relatives and *bozu*.

"*Namu Amida Butsu! Namu Amida Butsu!*" they solemnly repeated.

The flames burnt fiercely and soon enveloped the square coffin.

"Now, boys," whispered the Professor, "we shall return home."

As they quitted the enclosure, Ichiro said,—

"To-morrow the son and his wife will come and rake the ashes to see if their father has left his soul-pills."

"His what?" demanded Fitz, chuckling.

Ichiro smiled and replied,—

"It is most amusing, still many Buddhists firmly believe that after a man is burnt, his soul, in the form of small glass globules or pills, which are said to cure any disease, remains in his ashes. Our friends are of that opinion, and will be on hand to-morrow to search for the precious relics."

"I believe the *bozu* throw atoms of glass into the fire," said Oto. "It is all nonsense, anyhow!"

"Some persons have enough silicious matter in them to make a number of globular pellets," observed the Professor. "Well, well, every nation has its superstitions."

"Will the son take the soul-pills?" asked Fitz.

BURNING A BODY.

"No," said Ichiro, with a snicker. "He will keep them in a crystal box. It is very rarely that they are found."

"Jeminy!" cried Fitz. "How comical! I thought he might take them for rheumatism. Your countrymen are so fond of strange remedies."

"Our strange remedies are not worse than many of your patent medicines," said Ichiro. "Very few of our people believe in such things. Now we are here, I would like to visit my ancestors' graves. I can see lanterns moving near them, and think it possible some member of my family may be worshipping there."

The moon had risen, and was flooding the scene with its glorious light, bringing out the dark fringes of the cypresses and the white tombstones in strong relief.

AT THE ANCESTRAL TOMB.

The party turned to the left, and presently reached a spot near a second temple, where they found quite a number of persons. The monuments were formed of two horizontal slabs, surmounted by a square pillar, rounded or pointed at the top. This bore the posthumous title of the deceased, which generally was a high-flown sentence such as, —

"*Calmly reposing noble soul.*"

It was not a name but a eulogy of the dead, and was

engraved in a peculiar character that puzzled the boys to decipher. On the second slab of each tomb were stone vases for flowers and a hollow for water.

"That is my uncle's grave," said Ichiro, "where my cousin and his wife are kneeling. Uncle died in April, and next month they will place the monument in its proper position. He was a good man, but he disliked foreigners."

"Guess he was what we call a Know-nothing," said Fitz.

"Indeed, he was very intelligent and well educated," quickly answered Ichiro. "He was only ignorant of the virtues of your honorable nation."

"Yes, he was what we used to call a Know-nothing," was the reply. "Many Americans once hated foreigners, as he did us, and were called by that title."

"Say, Oto," inquired Johnnie. "Why does that man carry his beads on his ear?"

"For the same reason that your book-keepers place their pens there," answered the Japanese. "To have them handy."

"Why did your cousins light those lanterns at the back of the tomb?" demanded Fitz.

Ichiro grinned.

"Tell me."

"To let uncle's spirit know they are here," said the boy.

"The moon is shining brightly enough," merrily observed Johnnie. "Isn't that sufficient light for the *inkiyo* (retired old gentleman)?"

"It is all foolishness, anyhow," muttered Ichiro. "Still I think it is only proper to visit the graves of our ancestors and friends, and to keep their tombs in nice order."

"I agree with you," said the Professor. "I am afraid young America has not much respect for the dead. Your custom of visiting the graves of your loved ones is beautiful, and should be retained."

After Ichiro had spoken to his relatives, the party quitted the spot; leaving the mourners to continue their prayers.

"What does that pickle-tub contain?" said Fitz, pointing to a strongly hooped vessel, before which a lamp was burning.

"It is a coffin," said Ichiro. "The son of the deceased is away, and it will not be disturbed until he returns to perform the ceremonies."

"Do you pack your people in tubs? And do you bury them?"

"Yes, we both burn and bury our dead," returned Ichiro. "Do you take us for savages?"

"Come, boys, don't quarrel," said the Professor.

"We are only arguing, Sir," respectfully answered Ichiro. "Your sons think it strange that we inter our dead in tubs. I consider it much better than packing them in boxes like dried fish, as the Chinese do."

They all laughed at this, and halting at a *chaya* (restaurant) ordered tea and refreshments.

It was a picturesque spot. A magnificent wisteria, supported by a bamboo frame, covered the front of the hut, the thatch of which was overgrown with green moss, and the ridge crowned with lovely irises. A rooster and hen, perched on the slope, uttered uneasy clucks, and two partly-dressed travellers, seated on a bench under the wisteria, shouted vociferously for more rice.

A spring of ice-cold water rose from the ground immediately in front of the veranda; the overflow rushing off with a cool, gurgling sound, and mixing with a stream that flowed near by and was crossed by a plank bridge.

These *chaya* merely provide food and a temporary resting-place for travellers, and are not inns.

The party watched the scene and saw a woman and child come for *saké*, and two coolies arrive and join the men on the bench. Then the Professor paid for their refreshments, and they returned by the light of the moon to Nagasaki.

On reaching home they found a lad amusing the ladies by performing the fan-dance.

He had wooden swords thrust in his belt, in the old fashion, and was dressed in a peculiar costume. The American boys watched his performance, which was a compromise between a dance and a hop, and Fitz said, in his usual outspoken way —

THE FAN-DANCE.

"Our jig-dancers would astonish you. Why don't you put some life into your steps?"

"Oh, he can do the Uzume" (goddess-dance), said the boy's mother. "Kihachi, put aside your fans and delight the foreign gentlemen."

The girl who played the *samisen*, touched the strings rapidly, and Kihachi started a caper that shook the room and raised a blinding cloud of dust from the mats. He yelled, shouted, screamed, leaped, whirled and pounded until he became exhausted, when his mother bowed, and said, —

"Honorable gentlemen from afar, now is the moment for your kind appreciation."

Fitz gave the boy a dollar; and after the performers had departed, said to Ichiro, —

"Is that how your goddess danced? Jeminy, she must have been crazy."

"Yes; that is a rude representation of the way in which Uzume danced before the gods," answered Ichiro. "Our legend runs thus: The sun-goddess, Amaterasu, was scared by her brother Sosanoo, who played her all manner of tricks. She retired to a cave, and left the earth in total darkness. The gods assembled; and Uzume, mounting on a round box, danced and made them laugh."

"No wonder," said Johnnie. "We know the story. Guess I'll go to bed, as I am very tired."

The next morning they bade adieu to Nagasaki, and amid the *sayonara* (farewells) of their host, hostess, and servants, started for Kokuro — Sallie on her pony, Mrs. Jewett riding in a *jin-riki-sha* (man-drawn carriage) that had arrived the day before from Tokio, and the Professor and boys on foot.

A number of coolies, laden with baggage, followed the party, which travelled slowly, and halted frequently during the heat of the day.

"Now," cried Fitz, "for some jolly adventures."

## CHAPTER VII.

### A PLEASANT JOURNEY.

The tea and porcelain of Hizen,
The obi (silk girdles) of Chikuzen,
Are all most excellent.
When you visit these provinces
Remember your friends. — JAPANESE POEM.

ON the morning of the last day of August, the travellers reached Saga, a large town in the province of Hizen.

Sallie had tamed Abraham Lincoln, who followed her like a dog; Mrs. Jewett was becoming used to the motion of the *jin-riki-sha*, and the Professor and the boys were, what Fitz termed, "as brown as nuts."

"We will halt here for breakfast," said the head of the party, as they reached a street lined with *yadoya* (inns). "I see some nice fish on the stalls, and the place promises to provide a good breakfast."

They entered one of the largest inns, and submitted to have their feet laved by the attendants, then, after exhibiting their passports to the police, proceeded to a private room, ordered food, and, seating themselves on the mats, watched the arrivals and departures at an establishment across the road.

It was a lively scene, and the shrill cries of the guests and replies of the pert waitresses greatly amused the travellers.

Presently two coolies, bearing a *kago* enveloped in a net, came along the street and deposited their vehicle in front of the house.

A YADOYA (INN).

Behind them, was the head-man of a village, walking with a very important air.

Their arrival created quite a flutter in the establishment, and everybody glanced at them.

"*Hai!*" cried the landlord. "So you have caught him at last, eh? Here, girls, bring the excellent head-man a cup of *saké* and some hot rice — quick!"

"Why, there is a man inside that net," observed Fitz.

"Yes," nodded Oto. "He is a great criminal, and has killed several persons. That notice on the board, hanging from the bearing-pole, says, — 'Seven-fields — charged with many crimes.'"

While the *kago* bearers were relacing their sandals, the head-man refreshed himself, and described how he had captured the prisoner.

"You need not crow," growled the caged bandit. "I was asleep when you pounced on me."

Everybody appeared glad to see the fellow there, and the waitresses derided him, saying, —

"Serve you right, you wretch; you ought to be tortured. You have kept us all in terror. Now you will be handed over to the authorities."

"Yes," said a woman perched on a horse, which was secured by fastening its halter to its off leg. "You robbed my husband, you rascal. Ah! I am glad to see you in there."

"Is that the notorious Seven-fields?" asked a lady of a man who was scowling at the prisoner.

"Yes, that is the demon," replied the person addressed, pointing at the brigand. "Look at him. Two years ago he robbed me of my hard-earned savings. *Yeh!* you scoundrel, I would like to give you a blow."

The prisoner laughed, and holding up his hands, which were bound with a rope, saucily answered, —

"I would give you a dozen, if I were free. It is brave work to insult an honest man who is caged like a fox."

"*Yeh — yeh — yeh!*" shouted the guests.

When the *kago* was raised, and the bearers were moving off toward the police-court, the guests united in hooting the prisoner; even an old fish-vender, who was cleaning flounders on the sidewalk, joined in the cries, saying, —

"They ought to kill you on the spot; then we should be sure you would not rob any more of us."

The boys stepped into the kitchen, where they found the landlord and his wife eating breakfast, and chatting with a lightly-clad coolie, who was clinging to the door-post and telling the story of the thief's capture.

Behind the host were three pretty waitresses, listening to the recital, though they pretended not to be paying any attention to it.

"Killed a thousand people, did you say?" cried the host. "Nonsense!"

The coolie grinned, nodded, and said, —

"Well, honorable sir; he killed fifty with his own hand, and frightened nine hundred and fifty to death. It took a country-fellow to capture him. *Yeh*, these new policemen, with their foreign uniforms, are no good."

"Your guests, from afar, require you," said a stout man, who sat next to the host.

"We only want to learn something about the criminal," said Fitz. "He appeared to be a saucy fellow."

"He lived up in the mountain beyond," said the coolie. "I hear you require runners for your *jin-riki-sha*. Myself and brother are very anxious to go to Kokura. Will you engage us?"

The boys found that the men who had brought the vehicle from Nagasaki were lame, so they hired the applicants.

"What disease is that on your body?" asked Fitz; when the fellows stripped for work.

"Tattooing," replied the younger, as they turned and exhibited their backs. "We were formerly grooms in the service of Satzuma; now we are willing to do anything for an honest living."

A GOSSIPING COOLIE.

"You must wear clothes when you are with us," said Johnnie. "That decoration may be enough covering for you, but will not be sufficient for us."

The men bowed good-humoredly, and went off to fetch their best clothes; presently reappearing, dressed in neat cotton uniforms, marked with the crest of their late lord.

Johnnie and Fitz returned to their party, whom they found enjoying an excellent repast of fried fish, tea, and boiled rice.

"We've hired two of Barnum's tattooed men to draw you, mother," said Johnnie. "I tell you they are muscular fellows, and will spin you along two-ten."

TATTOOED FETTO (GROOMS).

The Professor, who was much interested in the old customs of the people, went out into the yard to see the men, who were busily employed washing the *jin-riki-sha*, and had again cast aside their garments. Directly they saw him they hastily caught up their clothes; noticing which he bade them have no fear, and inquired if they would mind his examining the tattooing on their bodies.

He asked so many questions that one of the coolies whispered to the other,—

"Our new master is a doctor. We shall be able to obtain his advice gratis."

This caused the gentleman to laugh, and he observed,—

"If you are sick, my young friend, Oto, will attend to you. I am not a physician."

"Then he is a magician," said the other coolie to his brother in a low aside. "Mind he does not take our strength from us."

After ascertaining their height and the measurement of their limbs and bodies, the Professor told them they need not be afraid, that he was neither a magician nor a quack doctor; on hearing which they bowed and resumed their work.

The ladies, feeling somewhat tired, rested while the gentlemen of the party went for a ramble about the town.

A GIRDLE DYER.

Every other house appeared to be inhabited by silk-weavers, and the clatter of the looms was heard on all sides.

The strangers stopped to see a man dyeing *obi* (ladies' silk girdles). He worked in the open air, and used the leaves that fell from the tree above his head as stamps. His only implements were a bucket containing dye, the leaves, and some sticks, between which were stretched the long pieces of white silk. He sang as he worked, and appeared to be perfectly happy.

One district of the town was inhabited by cotton-spinners,

and the travellers learned that much of the silk thread used for fabrics is only cotton plated or covered with silk.

They entered a large establishment devoted to the preparation of the staple, and found a number of women bowing the fibre, which was of good length and fine quality.

WOMAN BOWING COTTON.

The apparatus they used was a piece of bent bamboo and a strong cord, to which was attached a heavy bar of wood, forming the frame for a string of gut that was the bow of the machine.

The operator placed the raw cotton on a mat beneath the bow, and struck the string with a sort of mallet; the vibrations shaking the cotton into a fine down, and separating it from foreign matters and impurities.

Some of the women were turning rollers, on which the

bowed fibre was made into batting, and all of them were as white as though they had been in a snow-storm.

The proprietor of the establishment was formerly a *daimio* (lord), but had lost his title in the late political changes. He was very polite to his visitors, and showed them all over his factory, which a few years ago had been the mansion of another noble.

In the rear-yard they saw a man, perched high up on a sloping log, industriously sawing the timber with a primitive-looking instrument.

SAWING TIMBER.

The Japanese do not use saw-pits, nor have they yet, except in government establishments, adopted steam-saws. Labor is cheap, and the people object to foreign machinery.

"How long will he be cutting up that log?" asked Fitz.

"Probably a week," said the proprietor.

"Jeminy!" murmured the lad. "In America we would put that in a mill, and rip it into planks in ten minutes."

The sawyer, who overheard this remark, paused in his occupation, and rolling his eyes, whispered to a fellow-workman,—

"Did you hear him? He is making fun of us. We know better than to believe such idle stories."

The proprietor and his visitors smiled, and the former remarked,—

"Even I, who have read of such things, can scarcely credit them. I suppose you can do anything by machinery?"

"No," said the irrepressible Fitz. "You cannot convince people by its means."

"I think you can," slily observed Oto. "If this gentleman

could see a steam-saw at work, he would be convinced fast enough."

"Got me there," said Fitz, chuckling.

"What is that tinkling noise?" asked Johnnie. "It sounds like sleigh-bells."

"It proceeds from the Shinto temple near by," replied the manufacturer. "If you like, I will take you to the shrines. I know the *bozu* very well."

SHINTO TEMPLES.

"Are you a Shintoist?" inquired the professor.

The gentleman answered in the affirmative, when his interlocutor asked in what the religion consisted.

This evidently puzzled him; however, he presently said, —

"We term it *kami no michi* (the way of the gods). It teaches us to revere the Mikado (emperor), and to worship the unseen deities."

"How many Shinto gods are there?" demanded Fitz.

"About eight millions," was the calm reply. "Each spot and village has its own deity. We worship them all."

"We only believe in one God," said Johnnie.

The merchant smiled pityingly, and led the way through a lovely garden into a paved enclosure, in which stood two buildings of plain white wood. The roof of the smaller one was shingled, and that of the larger edifice thatched with grass.

In front of the former was a *torii* (pronounced toree) of white wood; two vertical posts crossed by a horizontal one and a narrow joist.

Johnnie eyed this structure, then remarked,—

"It only wants the inscription, 'Look out for the engine,' to be just like the notice-boards on our railway crossings. What does it mean?"

"*Torii* means bird-rest," said the manufacturer. "The original ones were formed of three sticks, put up before the Shinto shrines as rests for the birds that were offered, but not sacrificed, to the gods."

Upon the right of the *torii* was a huge lantern, and a roofed cistern filled with holy water, above which white cloths were suspended.

Their guide, who evidently wished to impress his foreign companions, advanced to the cistern, and, dipping his fingers in the water, touched his eyes and lips. Having done this, he ascended the steps of the shrine, and, seizing a piece of strong cotton cloth, attached to a bell fastened to the eaves, pulled it vigorously, then knelt, clapped his hands thrice, and bowed his head.

"He is praying for us," said Oto.

"Why did he clap his hands?" asked Fitz.

"To announce his presence to the gods," whispered their

friend. "This is a very silly faith, and no sensible person believes in it."

The worshipper rose, threw some money on to a white cloth inside the shrine, and after pointing to a wooden wand from which a number of notched papers were suspended, said in a low tone, —

"That is the *gohei* (sacred emblem). The gods come where it is exhibited."

"I want to know," murmured Fitz. "I thought it was a scarecrow. I've seen it stuck up in the fields."

"Fitz, be more reverential," said the Professor, in English. "Remember that gentleman believes in those things."

"Well — I don't, papa," answered the boy.

They passed under two other *torii*, one of which was decorated with a straw rope, fringed, like the *gohei*, with notched papers (another Shinto emblem).

"Do you worship those *gohei?*" demanded John.

"No," said their guide. "We worship the unseen gods."

"It does not look like it," muttered the boy.

The party advanced up a flight of steps at the foot of which were two hideous figures.

"Are those also Shinto emblems?" inquired Johnnie.

"No, they are Buddhist ones," replied the manufacturer. "We often attract outsiders to our faith by using their symbols. They are sky-dogs."

"They are of a very comical breed," said Fitz. "They have mouths like hippopotami."

On the top of the steps was a metal mirror in a frame (another Shinto emblem). This, and several large *gohei*, and some boards inscribed with a prayer, were all that was to be seen in the second temple.

A straw rope was suspended from the eaves of the structure, which was, like the first, a mere shed.

The visitors were about to retire, when a *bozu*, wearing a quaintly-formed cap, entered with a drum, followed by a girl, dressed in white, who bore a *gohei*, and carried a cluster of bells, fastened together like a child's toy-rattle.

SHINTO PRIEST AND PRIESTESS.

He squatted and watched the vestal, who, advancing to the mirror, chanted something in a quavering voice, and jingled the bells; whereupon the *bozu* beat his drum vigorously, with two thin sticks, and howled a response.

"That is the priestess who has custody of the mirror," whispered their guide. "This shrine is a copy of the one at Ize."

When the girl had retired, the *bozu*, whose head was not shaven like a Buddhist's, offered the visitors some tiny charms, of porcelain, shaped like a *torii*, remarking,—

"These will cure any disease."

"How many do you take at a time?" demanded Fitz, eying the articles suspiciously. "I should say they would be awkward to swallow."

The man laughed, and quickly answered,—

"That depends on how many you can afford to buy. Though I doubt if they will do you much good."

"Why not?" asked the boy.

"You do not believe in them, therefore they would not help you,—besides you ought to wear them in your girdle." Then he laughed, and said: "How does your honorable nation exist without believing in charms?"

The Professor briefly explained his faith, when the *bozu* scratched his left ear, and murmured,—

"Yes, yes! That is all very beautiful, but if I believed it, I should lose my means of existence, and my wife and children would have to starve. I am not one of those who jump in the dark."

This conversation evidently annoyed their guide, who, turning his back on the speaker, said,—

"Come, honorable sirs, I would like to offer you some very nice tea, grown in this province, and show you my garden."

As they quitted the temple-grounds they saw a bearded man and a ruddy-faced woman, watching them intently.

"Those are Ainos from the Island of Yezo," said the manufacturer. "They are only animals, anyhow."

The man referred to wore an enormous hat, and had a rude wallet suspended from his neck. The woman's head was bound with a towel, and she was nicely dressed in Japanese costume.

"The Ainos are supposed to be the aborigines of Japan," said Oto. "I never saw one before. The men all grow beards like foreigners!"

"Yes, they are mere animals," repeated the guide. "They run wild like tigers. I know all about them, my father visited their *ken*" (province).

"Why do you not wear a beard?" inquired Fitz.

"Because — because I—" began the gentleman, glancing at Oto.

AINOS FROM THE ISLAND OF YEZO.

"Because you cannot," slily answered the boy, who evidently resented the others remarks. "Honorable sir, you forget that his sacred Majesty, the Mikado, wears one!"

"Pardon me, I did not remember that," said the other. "Here is my house, allow me to have the honor of offering you some refreshments."

He led the way indoors and introduced them to his children, who were busily engaged playing battledore and shuttlecock.

The Japanese toy differs from ours, the bat being of light wood covered with paper, and the shuttle of pith and the same material.

Fitz and Johnnie examined the toy, and played a game with the youngsters, and when they had partaken of their host's hospitality, the Professor said,—

"Boys, we must say adieu and return to the inn. It is time for us to resume our journey."

BATTLEDORE AND SHUTTLE.

By four o'clock the party was once more *en route*, and about five reached the crest of the Hizen range, and saw the sunset illuminating the distant hills of Chikuzen. They paused in order to enjoy the lovely scene, and Sallie, pointing to a canal in the distance, said,—

"Why is that cut through there? I can see plenty of water on the right and left of it."

"It is the White-water canal," replied one of the coolies. "That river on the right is full of rapids. It is the outlet of the Chikugo."

After admiring the beautiful tints on the hills, they descended into the valley of Yakuna, a wild region sparsely clothed with trees.

The road was hewn through the living rock, and was cut in steps, which made the last part of the day's journey very tedious.

On the side of one pass they saw a slab, inscribed with the Buddhist prayer.

"Three years ago, a blind shampooer was robbed and murdered there," said one of the coolies.

"Are your unfortunates often thus ill-treated," asked Fitz.

"*Hai*," was the laughing response. "Those fellows always have plenty of money in their pouches. The one who said his final *Namu* there, had over a thousand dollars about him. He was, like most of his kind, a money-lender, and had, in his day, taken the last *sen* from many an honest man. I hate money-lenders; I have had one on my back for ten years."

"Why did you get in his debt?" demanded Johnnie.

"I used to drink too much *saké*," sighed the coolie. "Ah! I have been very foolish. *Saké* is a very bad thing. I suppose your honorable countrymen are all temperate?"

"I'm afraid not," said Fitz.

Just before dusk they came to an old tree enclosed with a railing. The trunk bristled with nails to which hung fragments of paper and rags.

In front of the tree was a Shinto shrine and a Buddhist *torii*, the latter being painted a dull red. A curious mixture of the symbols of the rival faiths of the people.

The tattooed runners, who dragged Mrs. Jewett's *jin-riki-sha*, and the coolies who bore the baggage, halted and entering the enclosure, rubbed their hands on the bark of the tree, then applied them to various parts of their bodies.

The travellers watched them in amazement, and Fitz said, "Why do you do that?"

"This is a sacred tree," said one of the men. "We always give it a trial, so if we are not cured it is no fault of ours."

Then he laughed and said to his companions: "Come, comrades, that rub will enable us to reach the inn of the 'Seven Beautiful Scenes.'"

"One moment," said the amused boy; "why are those nails driven all over the trunk of the tree?"

"Ask your honorable friend there," answered the man. "He can tell you better than I. He used to believe in such things."

"I am sure I never did," muttered Otto.

As they resumed their journey he said,—

"These nails were driven in the tree by ignorant persons who desired to be revenged on their enemies. Your ancestors used to do something of the kind."

"Yes, but we do not," quickly retorted Fitz.

"No," quietly retorted Oto. "When your bad people take a dislike to any one they shoot them down; ours merely make a paper figure of the object of their hatred and nail it to a tree. The act relieves their feelings, and does not hurt their would-be victim."

"*Hai!*" screamed Sallie, pointing to a strange object on the roadside. "There is a robber aiming a bow and arrow at me. Hai!"

The coolies stopped, and laughingly demolished the "brigand," which proved to be a scarecrow, made of an old *mino* (straw-coat), a tattered bamboo hat, and three sticks.

"Oh, how it scared me!" said Sallie. "The girls at the inn told us such dreadful stories about robbers. I thought that was one."

A PRIMITIVE SCARECROW.

It soon became too dark to make out the way, so they halted at the door of a farm-house and asked to be accommodated for the night.

The farmer was very hospitable, and gave them the best his house afforded.

He ordered his wife and daughter to dress in their holiday costumes, and, donning his silken suit, waited on the visitors.

When they had ended their supper he took some of the remains on a small tray, and, squatting in a corner, ate, smoked, drank, and plied his guests with questions; his family listening to the replies with unmoved faces, evidently deeming it would not be good manners to join in the conversation.

He wanted to know almost as badly as Fitz, and had his guests not yawned repeatedly behind their fans, would have talked all night.

. THE FARMER AND HIS FAMILY.

Finally, he bade his wife put up the screens, and when the room was divided into four compartments, retired to the smallest with his silent companions.

None of the party enjoyed much sleep, as the mats on the floor swarmed with bloodthirsty insects: added to which annoyance, a rattling noise proceeded from a field at the back of the house. When the Jewetts rose they discovered that the sound came from pieces of hard wood strung with short sticks of bamboo. These were suspended from strings, moved by the breeze, which rattled them like old windows in a gale, and effectually scared the birds off the newly sown ground.

While the ladies were making their toilets, the gentlemen watched a wood-cutter and a charcoal-vender, who were discussing the advent of foreigners in the district. The wood-cutter leaned on an enormous axe, and talked in a loud voice, and his companion, who was seated on the ground, resting against his charcoal-baskets, smoked, and replied in a very comical treble.

A BIRD-RATTLER.

"Yes, they are strange people," shouted the wood-cutter who did not know the farmer's guests were out and about. "I am waiting to see them. The time I shall lose will be well spent. I hear that the man and boys have long hair on their heads, like monkeys, and that the elder of the ladies has never dyed her teeth. They are only half-civilized. What do you think they are doing in our honorable country?"

CHARCOAL-SELLER AND WOOD-CUTTER.

The charcoal-seller, who knew the foreigners were listening, rolled his eyes comically and replied, —

"I hear they have come to buy timber."

"That is good news," said the woodman. "I ought to have spoken more respectfully of them."

"Hai!" shouted Fitz; "won't you come and speak to us monkeys?"

The man turned, advanced, knelt and bowed respectfully, then said, —

"A thousand pardons for my rudeness. Honorable sirs, I am only an ignorant wood-cutter. My name is Koshima. I can supply you with timber at a reasonable price."

"My good friend, we are merely travelling for pleasure," smilingly observed the Professor. "We are not here to buy logs."

The disappointed man bowed, and returned to the laughing charcoal-vender, whom he thus addressed:

"Matsu-moto, I have known you many years, and did not think you would thus shame my face before those honorable gentlemen from afar. Hai! you may laugh; but I feel like a toad that has attempted to swallow a hornet."

The spectators imagined he would strike the joker; however, he merely scowled at him, shouldered his axe, and walked off. Japanese peasants seldom come to blows, and are, as a body, quiet, good-tempered people.

Although the farm-yard was full of chickens, the mistress of the house declined to kill any of them, saying, —

"Honorable sirs, you are welcome to what my house affords, but my religion forbids me to take life. How should I be able to look those good creatures in the face after I had murdered one of their number?"

When the Professor asked how much there was to pay, the farmer said, —

"Nothing. I do not keep an inn. May you live long, enjoy good health, and be spared to return to your honorable parents. I wish you a pleasant journey."

Mrs. Jewett gave their hostess some needles, and Sallie added a pair of American scissors which the daughter had greatly admired. Then the travellers said *sayonara*, and resumed their journey.

A PLEASANT JOURNEY.

The heat was intense; spite of which, the men who dragged the *jin-riki-sha* ran it up the hills, and raced Sallie's pony on the level ground; sometimes returning a mile or two, in order to keep company with the pedestrians.

The fourth day after leaving the farm, they arrived at Kokura, in the province of Hizen, which they reached about sunset. When they had eaten supper, and exhibited their

BLESSING THE WATER.

passports to the police, who called to know their names, &c., they went out on the ramparts to witness a *Shinto* ceremony, which Oto termed " Blessing the Water."

Three *bozu*, dressed in white, squatted on a mat behind a low table, festooned with strips of notched paper, before them being a frame containing four small *gohei*.

Four bamboos, bearing lanterns, were erected at regular

distances, and the space was enclosed with cleft sticks, in each of which was a folded paper.

On the right was a stone lantern that gave out a red light, and on each side were platforms occupied by well-dressed spectators, and by tea, cake, and *saké* sellers, who drove a brisk trade.

Persons using the seats paid extra, and put on more airs than those who squatted on the bare ground.

The sea broke with a loud roar on the beach below, children laughed and screamed, the women and men chattered and smoked, amid which din the *bozu* calmly chanted, rang their bells, and waved their *gohei;* pausing every now and then while their assistants collected the offerings of the faithful.

After the moon had risen, the *bozu* prostrated themselves, then rose, advanced to the edge of the ramparts, and threw hundreds of strips of paper into the water. That done, they formed in procession and marched homeward, the people following in a mob and shouting vociferously.

"What does it all mean?" asked Fitz.

"Nothing," replied Oto. "It is a mere ceremony, the origin of which has long ago been forgotten."

"Oto," said Johnnie, "you say no sensible Japanese believes in Buddhism or Shintoism. Now, I have seen a great many of your countrymen and women, but have only met a few like yourself."

The boy thought for a moment, and quietly replied, —

"Wait until you get to Tokio. Out of a thousand Americans how many are really sensible persons, like your folks? I met with people in your country who believed in worse nonsense than Buddhism or Shintoism."

"That is true," said Johnnie. "There are the Mormons, for instance. Well, your countrymen and women are real kind, gentle people, and have treated us first-rate."

Early the next morning they went on the ramparts for a walk, and beheld, across the straits, the town of Shimonoseki. "I have friends over there," said Oto. "It is the place that, in 1863, was bombarded by the allied forces; for which little attention we had to pay your country seven hundred and eighty-five thousand dollars."

"What?" cried the boys. "You had to pay us for killing your people. Why, that's absurd."

SHIMONOSEKI FROM THE HEIGHTS OF KOKURA.

"So we have always thought," was the quiet response. "The lord of Magato was ordered by the authorities to prevent foreign ships from anchoring off Shimonoseki. Although both your honorable nation, the English, French and Dutch knew of this, they persisted in disregarding the notification; consequently whenever their ships approached the batteries of Shimonoseki they were fired at, the first discharges always being blank ones. Several engagements occurred between our batteries and ships and the foreign vessels of war, and, finally, the allied fleet, —

THE TOWN OF SHIMONOSEKI.

THE RUINS OF THE FORTS OF SHIMONOSEKI.

consisting of one American vessel, hired for the occasion and armed with one gun, nine British, four Dutch and three French vessels of war,—assembled off Shimonoseki, and began to bombard the batteries and town."

"I remember seeing a picture of the smoking ruins in a book of yours," said Sallie. "When I asked you what it was you tore it up."

"Yes," gravely answered Oto. "I had kept it to remind me of the desolation wrought by the allies, of our dead patriots, ruined homes and shattered forts. I destroyed it in order to banish the affair from my mind."

"And do you mean to say, sir," said Johnnie to his father, "that after taking such a revenge we made the Japanese pay for defending themselves?"

"Yes, to our shame, that is true," said the Professor. "We joined the English, French and Dutch in a disgraceful act, worthy of the dark ages, and extorted three millions of dollars from a nation in the throes of a civil war, sharing the plunder equally with our allies. The money we thus wrung from Japan still lies in our national treasury, and, with the interest, amounts to over a million of dollars."

"Papa," said Fitz, "are you sure somebody has not appropriated it? If it is still there, it ought to be returned."

"It is safe enough," smilingly replied the Professor. "Congress alone has the power to restore it to its lawful owners."

"We have never asked for it," said Oto. "We paid what England, America, France and Holland demanded in order to avoid more trouble, but had our own opinion about the matter."

. "Congress ought to see to that," said Sallie, who was intensely interested in the narration.

"You just wait until I am a member," said Fitz; "I'll fix that Shimonoseki matter, Oto."

"I guess we shall have to wait as long," was the significant reply.

They watched the ships moving through the Strait. Then, after paying their coolies and visiting the principal places in Kokura, hired a passage-boat to convey them and their effects to the opposite shore.

A PASSENGER-BOAT.

The craft was sculled by six men, who jointly owned her, and was as clean as a new pin. In the centre was a commodious cabin, and in the bow a wooden anchor. All the woodwork was unpainted, and not a nail was used in her construction, every part being either pegged or dovetailed together.

The voyagers embarked and, when the *jin-riki-sha*, Sallie's pony, and the baggage, had been taken on board, were swiftly rowed over the blue water toward the ancient port of Shimonoseki, whose batteries gleamed white in the distance.

The waves lapped idly against the bows, and the sea-birds, sailing overhead, uttered shrill cries, as though welcoming the young Americans to Hondo, the main island of the Japanese Empire.

"Sallie," said Mrs. Jewett, glancing at the thoughtful face of her daughter, "of what are you thinking?"

"I know," cried Fitz. "She is thinking what a jolly long while it is since we had a square meal."

Sallie bit her lips, for her brother had guessed the truth.

"Here comes a fune (junk)," shouted Johnnie, pointing ahead. "Is she not a regular Noah's ark?"

The travellers peeped out of the cabin-windows, and saw a strange-looking craft bearing down upon them.

JAPANESE JUNK.

## CHAPTER VIII.

OTO'S MANLY AVOWAL.

His mother wept and prayed,
His friends frowned upon him,
But he was firm, and said:
"I cannot pretend to believe
What I know is false and foolish."
     ' JAPANESE HISTORY OF A CONVERT.

THE *fune* (junk), like the passenger-boat, was built of unpainted wood, and was a good specimen of the old style craft of Japan. Its massive mast was composed of pieces of timber dovetailed and pegged together, and its bow was decorated with an enormous tassel of fibre. This, Oto said, was intended for a fender, to prevent the vessel from damaging another in a collision. It had a gigantic rudder-post, a strong rudder, and a large, square sail, made of stout cotton cloth.

On nearing the boat, the *fune* tacked and sailed off at an angle; the crew shouting at the rowers of the passenger-craft, and pointing to a fleet of foreign-built vessels anchored before the town.

"They are calling our attention to the ships of the Imperial navy," said Oto proudly. "We have, in proportion to our population, a larger army and navy than the United States."

"You require it," said Fitz. "England and Russia would both like to annex you, and, if you had no war establishment, China would hold you in contempt. We Americans are so powerful that no nation dare molest us, so we do not require a large army and navy."

"China!" indignantly retorted Oto. "Why, we could whip her any day! When she was unable to put down the pirates in Formosa we organized an expedition and wiped them out. China! We do not fear her any more than you do Great Britain."

"Good boy," laughingly observed the Professor. "I like to hear any one defend his country."

The fleet, which consisted of ten vessels, presented a very warlike appearance, and was a credit to its officers, all of whom were Japanese.

A number of small steamers, used in the coasting-trade, were lying off the town, and inshore were some trading crafts of the old build and rafts of timber. The place had a desolate air, as though business had departed from it, and there was little of the noise and bustle they had heard on the wharves of Kokura.

The travellers disembarked, and when the pony, *jin-riki-sha* and luggage were landed, and the Professor satisfied the police that they were not dangerous characters or traders, he said,—

"Now, Oto, where shall we go? Is there a good hotel in the town?"

"You had better stay here in the Custom House while I visit my friends," he replied.

"Can't we accompany you?" urged Johnnie.

Oto shook his head.

"You need not be ashamed if they are poor," said the irrepressible Fitz. "We have no false pride about us."

Oto chuckled, and again shook his head.

"Come," cried Johnnie, "I am going with you, anyhow."

"I believe his pretty cousin, O-Kiku, lives here," said Sallie. "May I go with you, boys?"

This speech made Oto laugh, and he replied,—

"Cousin Kiku lives in Nikko. I will tell you the trut' My friends here are my cousin and uncle, who are Buddhi *bozu*. If you go with me, boys, you must not ridicule wh; you see. They believe in Buddha."

"What?" said Fitz. "You have relatives who are Buddhist *bozu*?"

"Why not?" queried the boy. "You have a relation who is a Catholic priest, and another who is a Baptist minister."

Sallie laughed merrily, and Johnnie said, —

"You are right, Oto. We will promise to keep our opinions to ourselves. I am afraid we have let our tongues run rather freely. You always expressed so much contempt for Buddhism that we have said just what we thought about it."

"You know I do not believe in it," he quietly replied. "What I am afraid of is Fitz saying something that will hurt my relatives' feelings. Uncle is an aged man, and has always been very good to me."

"Don't you worry," said the boy. "I'll treat the *inkiyo* (retired old gentleman) respectfully.".

The friends entered a boat, and were rowed to a landing-place about a mile from the Custom House.

"That is the entrance to the temple of which my uncle is Sojo," said Oto, pointing to a *torii* which stood inside a railing on a neatly-kept wharf. "Those sky-dogs came from China, and, with the stone lanterns, were gifts from the late lord of the province."

"Why has that *torii* a centre-piece between the two horizontal ones?"

"I do not know," answered Oto. "You only see it on Buddhist *torii*. I believe it is merely to strengthen the structure."

They ascended the steps, and found themselves on a broad plateau, above which was a second *torii* and two flights of steps; one steep and straight, and the other winding in and out on the hillside.

On their right was a spring of mineral water, and a shrine covered with straw shoes left by persons who had been cured by drinking the nauseous liquid, which smelt strongly of sulphur.

Near by was a shed devoted to the sale of charms, sandals, and *saké* (rice wine).

THE LONG FLIGHT OF STEPS.

"Jeminy!" grumbled Fitz. "Why don't they have an inclined tramway, the same as at Niagara Falls. Must we climb all those steps?"

"Oh, that is only a short flight," laughingly answered Oto. "At Kamakoura they have one twice as high. This is nicely shaded, and pilgrims often ascend and descend it a hundred times."

"They must be lunatics," growled Fitz.

THE TORII AT THE LANDING-PLACE.

After many pauses they reached the top step, and saw on a level ground before them a bell-tower and temple.

"Why, that tower is the brother of the one at Nagasaki," said Johnnie.

"Yes, the Nagasaki tower and monument were copied from this one."

"I would like a cup of water," grumbled Johnnie, who was perspiring freely. "My! is not the sun hot?"

To the left was a handsome lantern of stone, which Oto said was erected to one of the lords of Nagato who had renounced his title and died a *bozu*. Behind this were three stone cisterns containing holy-water.

The place was neatly paved with marble, and contained many beautiful lanterns of bronze and granite, erected to the memory of nobles who had long been forgotten by the people.

The main temple had a high-pitched roof, the ridge-board of which bore the *mon* (crest) of three great lords. A Shinto bell hung from the eaves of the porch, and a representation of a mirror was carved on the woodwork of the eaves.

"How quiet the place is!" said Johnnie. "It really feels like a sacred spot. Even the doves up there among the carvings of the roof are silent."

"It is too precious hot for them to be cooing," grumbled Fitz. "Say, Oto, in which building does your uncle live."

"Not in this temple," he slily answered.

They put off their shoes and entered the edifice, when they were accosted by a young *bozu*, who said to Oto, in excellent English,—

"Hello! old man, where did you spring from?"

This sounded so comical from the lips of a shaven-headed *bozu* that Johnnie exclaimed, —

"Where did you learn to speak our language?"

"In America," replied the *bozu*, who was shaking hands

with their companion. "I suppose you are the Mr. Jewetts of whom I have often heard?"

"This is my cousin Ikeda," said Oto, introducing his friends. "He is the nephew of my uncle Matsuo."

"Welcome to our temple," said the delighted *bozu*. "I resided some years in the States. How are things there? Is the election decided? You see I live apart from the world, and seldom receive news from home."

"Home!" echoed the Jewetts.

"Well, I meant the States," was the laughing response. "Come and have some tea and cakes. I am real glad to see you."

They quitted the temple and entered a courtyard, in which some *bozu* were taking exercise.

"Won't the bishop be astonished to see you?" remarked Ikeda, as he led the way past the silent group.

"Bishop?" queried John.

"Yes, bishop is the English equivalent for Sojo," was the merry answer. "Oto is a great favorite of our uncle. I am sure you will like our relative; he is a very noble and venerable man. He sent me to the States, and has done everything for me. This is my room."

He showed them into a small cell. There was no furniture on the bare floor; the only articles in the apartment being a lamp, a case of books and a few quilts.

Ikeda, who, spite of his shaven head was quite good-looking, sent for some refreshments, and lighting his pipe, rattled on in English, inquiring about old friends in the States, and imparting family news to Oto, who, spite of his cousin's cordial welcome, appeared dull and uncomfortable.

When the guests had partaken of the refreshments, Ikeda said,—

"Now, I will go to the bishop. He usually walks in the

grounds about this hour. I am sure he can tell you of a good
ice to lodge, he knows everybody."

As soon as the *bozu* had retired, Fitz said to Oto, —

"Why are you so glum. Were those steps too much for
you."

"I — I — never thought of this," murmured their friend.
He will of course expect I am as I was when I quitted him for
Tokio."

BOZU TAKING EXERCISE.

"Who — what — how?" coolly demanded Fitz. "What
are you muttering about?"

Oto shook his head, and nervously rubbed his hands one
over the other, then said in a low tone, as though fearing
Ikeda was listening, —

"I never gave it a thought until I saw my cousin."

"Are you going crazy?" inquired Fitz.

"What is the matter?" asked Johnnie.

"Boys," whispered the perplexed youth, "what am I to do? When I last saw my uncle I was a Buddhist,— now—"

"Won't he give you pepper," said Fitz. "Of course you will not pretend to believe that superstitious nonsense, just to please him?"

"I wish I were a thousand miles away," moaned Oto. "I shall not say I believe in Buddhism, yet, — I hate to grieve my uncle."

"Does he believe in it?" asked Johnnie.

"Most assuredly he does," said their friend. "Well, — I shall tell the truth."

"That is right," said Johnnie. "Here comes Ikeda."

"The bishop is anxious to see you," said the young *bozu*. "He is in the garden. Come with me."

They passed through a corridor, in which sat three young *bozu* eating their midday meal of plain boiled rice.

"We never see tenderloin steak here," said Ikeda. "At first, after I returned from the States, I felt a craving for animal food, but now I have conquered the desire. You will soon do the same, cousin Oto."

The latter murmured something and bit his lips. He knew that his uncle's first question would be whether he had remained true to the teachings of his youth.

"Do you live entirely on rice and vegetables?" asked Johnnie of Ikeda. "Are you never permitted to eat eggs or fish?"

"Certainly not," gravely answered the young *bozu*. "When I was in America I had a dispensation to eat anything; however, on my return, I resumed the correct way of living. I see Oto has not converted you to our faith."

"Not by a large majority," said Fitz. "I thought no sensible Japanese believed in Buddhism."

Oto frowned at him, but he might as well have made a signal to the sun to cease shining.

Ikeda laughed good-humoredly, and replied, —

"Every one has his own belief. Ours forbids us to eat anything that has lived. Hush, there is the bishop."

They halted and beheld, at a little distance from them, an aged man, whose wrinkled face, eyebrows and head were shaven, and were of a uniform waxen yellow tint.

BOZU AT DINNER.

In his right hand he carried a fan; in his left, which was partly concealed by the sleeve of his white robe, was a rosary of crystal beads; and over his costume was a circular stole of silk, embroidered with the Buddhist prayer. His feet were encased in cotton *tabi* (socks), and he wore broad clogs of white wood.

Although his features were heavy, and somewhat coarse in outline, he had a dignified, benevolent look, and impressed the boys very favorably.

Oto trembled when he saw his relation, and, falling upon his hands and knees, bowed his head to the ground.

Ikeda also prostrated himself, but Johnnie and Fitz remained standing, and merely bowed politely.

"Welcome to Shimonoseki," said the old man, in a pleasant tone. "I trust your honorable parents are in the enjoyment of good health."

Fitz advanced, extended his hand, and said,—

"They are quite well, thank you, Bishop! How are you?"

The Sojo smiled, and, taking his hand, replied,—

"I thank you for your kind inquiry. So you have brought back my nephew. We are much indebted to you for all your goodness to him."

He then shook hands with Fitz and

OTO'S UNCLE.

Johnnie, after which he turned to Oto, who still kept his head on the ground, and said, —

"My son, I hope you have not lost faith in Buddha."

Oto did not reply.

"I hear," continued the venerable man, "that nearly all our students who go abroad return with changed hearts. I trust you have not forgotten the doctrines of our holy faith."

Poor Oto! he feared he was about to separate himself from his family, — to become an object of detestation to them. He was too noble to lie, so, rising, he bowed in foreign fashion, and, facing his amazed relative, said, —

"Honorable uncle, since I last beheld your face I have learned many things. I no longer believe in the teachings of my childhood."

Instead of being angry, the Sojo exclaimed, —

"Alas! alas! I feared it was so. I will pray that you may be brought to see the error of your ways and be restored to reason. Your mother will indeed feel grieved when she hears this bad news."

He turned away, and walked slowly toward his cell, sobbing as he went.

When his uncle was out of sight, Ikeda rose and said, —

"Oto, you are a true man! I believe just as you do, but have not dared to own it?"

The Sojo sent for them after a little while, and, without referring to his nephew's change of belief, inquired if he could do anything for him or his friends.

Oto answered that he was anxious to find accommodations for his party; on hearing which the Sojo wrote a note, and said, —

"Take this to Tamai Wage, on Saltfish Street; he will give you good rooms. There is no inn in the city fit to be the abode of the American ladies. Come and see me before you leave, and mind you think over what I have said."

He ordered refreshments to be brought, and chatted pleasantly with the Americans, who took a great liking to him.

"Excuse me," said Fitz, pointing to a *kakemono* (hanging picture) on the wall. "Why do you have the portrait of warrior in your room?"

The Sojo smiled, and gently replied,—

"That represents Kato Kiyomasa, who was a great general and a holy man. I thought all the world had heard of him."

The boy surveyed the painting, which depicted the bearded warrior in full armor, seated on his camp-stool; behind him being a banner inscribed with the prayer,—

"*Namu Amida Butsu.*"

When Fitz had examined every detail of the costume, he turned to the venerable man, who was regarding him out of the corners of his eyes, and coolly said,—

KATO KIYOMASA.

"Oh! that is Kato, is it? Hum! He was the individual who killed so many Christians, was he not?" adding, in a musing tone, "I don't like the cut of his Ulster."

"He is now a saint," said the Sojo.

He then dismissed them, and they quitted the temple grounds.

On reaching their boat, Oto said,—

"I am glad that interview is over. My worst trial will be with my mother. I have never referred to this matter in my letters, and fear she will be greatly grieved."

"Cheer up, old fellow," said Johnnie. "You must enlighten her. She is a sensible lady, and will listen to the truth from you. Anyhow, she'll forgive you — mothers always do."

"I hope so," said Oto with a sigh. "I think it better to say I do not believe in Buddhism than to do like my cousin Ikeda."

"Yes," said Fitz, "it is always best to speak the truth."

When the Professor heard of what had occurred, he said,—

"Oto, you behaved like a man. A person who pretends to believe what he knows in his heart is false, is beneath contempt. As to your parents, I am sure they will forgive you."

"My father will," quietly answered the noble fellow. "He has not much respect for Buddhism, but my honored mother has every faith in its teachings, and will, I am afraid, be terribly pained on discovering that I have none. My uncle is sure to write her all about it."

They comforted him, and, after having engaged runners for the *jin-riki-sha*, proceeded to Saltfish Street.

Mr. Tamai, a very pleasant gentleman, who had lost his fortune by the revolution, showed them a large room, which, he said, could be divided by screens into four apartments.

"How much is the rent per day?" inquired the Professor.

"Will a *yen* (dollar) be considered exorbitant?" he asked. "I will, for that sum, furnish you with any number of screens and with quilts for your beds. The ladies can have the use of our kitchen, and I will not charge you extra for fuel."

The bargain was soon closed, and the party and their belongings installed in their new abode.

Sallie and the boys went out marketing, and contrived to

## OTO'S MANLY AVOWAL.

secure a couple of chickens, some kidney potatoes, dried beans, salt and fresh fish, a squash, and a basket of lily-roots, which Oto said were very good to eat.

Upon their return they found the Professor and Mrs. Jewett in the kitchen, a dark apartment at the rear of the house.

The cooking apparatus consisted of a box, containing a huge earthen bowl partly filled with live charcoal.

"We have to keep fanning the coals with this," said the Professor, exhibiting a fan made of oiled paper. "I don't believe we shall ever raise enough heat to broil those chickens."

"Let me show you," said Oto, squatting near the box, and taking the fan from his friend. "There is a knack in lighting these fires."

He fluttered the article in a peculiar manner, which soon made the coal glow, and within ten minutes the mass was red hot.

JAPANESE COOK'S FAN.

Fitz and Johnnie killed and dressed the birds, and Mrs. Jewett superintended the cooking, the result being what her sons termed "a square meal."

To tell the truth, living in the Japanese style had proved rather unsatisfactory, and all of the party were glad enough to return to American cookery.

The next morning they had fish-balls and pork-and-beans for breakfast, after which they started to see the sights of Shimonoseki.

"Everybody appears to be in holiday attire," said Sallie.

"Yes," answered Oto. "This is a *matsuri* (festival), and I hear there is to be a grand procession in honor of a local deity."

"Do you want to buy tickets for good seats?" inquired a man, who carried a long string of bamboo tallies on his arm. "I can furnish you with places in a beautiful spot on the main street. Only ten *sen* each."

"So you have ticket-speculators in Japan," whispered Sallie.

"Oh, yes! We have most of the modern improvements," was Oto's ready rejoinder. "Shall I secure places?"

"If you please," answered the Professor. "We want to see all the sights."

Oto purchased tickets of admission to a shop close by, and in a few moments had his party seated.

On the other side of the road was a two-storied building crowded with sight-seers, and, on the corner of the street, a recess in which stood a large tub of water, surmounted by a pyramid of fire-buckets.

"That is one of our provisions against conflagrations," said Oto. "There is a similar arrangement in every street."

"Better have a fire-engine," remarked Fitz. "I don't call that thing a modern improvement."

On their left was a street, the houses of which were curtained with colored cotton drapery and filled with people, who smoked continually and chattered like magpies.

It was noon before the procession came in sight, and the spectators were growing weary of waiting.

First came a body of men dressed in quaint costumes. Oto said they were members of the various guilds, who had united to pay the expenses of the festival.

Following these were persons carrying spears and flags, and companies of men belonging to various religious associations.

The next feature of the affair was a clumsy, two-wheeled cart, surmounted by a draped framework, on which was a mound supporting three gigantic figures and a clump of fir-trees. Behind this group sat men beating drums and clashing cymbals.

"Whom does that bearded figure represent?" asked I.

"That is the god Takenouchi," returned Oto. "He is very popular in this part of the country.

The cart was drawn by two water-buffaloes, assisted by volunteers, who, from time to time, quitted the ranks of the

FESTIVAL IN HONOR OF TAKENOUCHI.

spectators and seized the drag-ropes. They yelled and shouted like sailors heaving up an anchor, and sometimes, in their eagerness, dragged both cart and buffaloes.

The managers of the procession wore hempen wings over their dresses, and were very haughty and self-important.

"Come," said Oto, after the cart had passed. "I know a place near here where we can get delicious fish-sausages and Ise ea Will you not try some?"

"I am willing," said Fitz.

"So am I," said Sallie. "I am both hungry and thirsty."

They quitted the shop, and followed him to a street lined with restaurants devoted to the sale of the luxuries he had mentioned.

"This is a celebrated house," he remarked, motioning them to enter a neatly-kept establishment, bearing the sign of "The Royal Carp." "I have eaten many a meal here."

They squatted on the matted floor, and watched the cooks mincing fish with large knives.

On the other side of the road was a rival concern, the proprietor of which was evidently annoyed at not having received the foreigners as customers. He stood in the front of his store and shouted, —

"This is the only place in the street where you can obtain genuine Yezo whale-flesh sausage. This is the original Royal Carp — all others are base imitations."

"Yeh," shouted their host, regarding him angrily. "Cease making that ugly noise, or you will lose the few patrons who are foolish enough to put up with your inferior wares. You know your Yezo whale-flesh is nothing but Yedo-bay shark."

"I only serve our honorable countrymen," derisively returned the other. "I don't keep a house of entertainment for Chinese."

Their altercation was cut short by the arrival of a dealer in second-hand clothes, who, depositing his wooden horse in the roadway, addressed them, saying, —

"Honorable sirs, don't waste your time in defaming one another, but bring out your old coats. I am in a hurry to get rid of my money."

This caused the sausage-makers and spectators to laugh, and secured the witty fellow a lady customer, who shouted at him as though he were deaf, saying, —

"I want a pair of trousers for my husband. None of your

old rags, mind. Give me something that was once worn by a nobleman."

"She evidently means to secure a bargain," remarked Jewett.

"Most ladies like to do so," quietly replied Oto.

"Look at that dear little baby tied to her back," cried Sallie. "Is he not 'cute?"

The child, who was about three years old, made a grimace at her, and shouted,—

"*Shu-ten-doji* (red-faced ghoul)!"

On hearing this, his mother sharply reprimanded him, observing,—

"You must not say such naughty things, or the *oni* (imps) will come for you. You should say *onna tojin* (foreign woman)."

This remark made the party laugh until their sides ached; it being about as comical as the mother of a Californian hoodlum scolding her son for calling a Celestial a "heathen Chinee," and bidding him address the man as a "benighted foreigner."

It was the first rude speech made to the Americans, and even then the woman did not intend to be impolite.

While the boys were commenting upon the incident, some waitresses entered with trays containing the specialty of the establishment; sausages of finely-minced fish, seasoned with herbs and fried in highly-colored paper envelopes.

"I supposed you would prefer these cooked," slily remarked Oto.

"Do you ever eat these raw?" asked Sallie.

"Yes," he merrily answered. "Do you not sometimes eat uncooked ham?"

"Not I," said the young lady. "I'm afraid of the *trichina*."

They laughed, chatted, enjoyed the repast, drank the delicious tea, and watched the scene on the street, where an acrobat, mounted on high clogs, and his assistant had collected a small crowd, consisting of two merchants, a servant-maid carrying a child, a domestic who had been purchasing sausages of the opposite maker, and three school-boys; one of whom had his books tied to his right wrist.

The performer fastened a horn to the back of his head, then tossed two cups and a bottle into the air, and caught them in the receptacle; repeating his feat with lightning rapidity.

A STREET PERFORMANCE.

His assistant beat a drum placed on a circular lantern, which bore the arms of an ex-noble, and yelled vociferously to his employer.

The exhibition greatly delighted the Japanese; even the man who tended the charcoal fire of the porcelain cooking-range, pausing in his occupation to watch the feats, which were loudly applauded by the school-boys.

The Professor gave the performer a few cents, and paid the bill for the refreshments, remarking, —

"Now we will visit the street of the dealers in bronz

They halted on their way to witness the tricks of a co who, squatting upon a mat, executed some marvellous feats of sleight-of-hand. Before him was a *sambo* (box with pierced sides used as a tray) supporting an empty bowl, and on his left lay a roll of plain white paper.

A CONJUROR.

He took a sheet of the latter, crumpled it up in his hand, and threw it into the bowl, then drew forth a long strip of colored ribbon, which he flourished overhead, shouting, —

"I am the marvellous magician, Kayai."

The crowd about him was too dense for the travellers to watch him with comfort, so they resumed their walk, presently arriving at their destination; a large street containing shops entirely devoted to the sale of bronze bowls, lanterns, and similar works of art.

Here five lightly-clad coolies were propelling a clumsy cart, on which rested an enormous bell that weighed at least a ton.

Although the Japanese government has forbidden people to go unclothed, it is not an uncommon sight to see coolies in dishabille; however, when the police *notice* the offenders they arrest them, and the law-breakers are heavily fined, and sometimes punished with imprisonment.

In the first shop were two ex-nobles, who, on seeing the Americans, turned and regarded them with haughty indifference.

Fitz, mistaking them for the proprietors, advanced, and said,—

"*Hai!* what do you ask for those bronze lanterns on the right of the entrance?"

This caused a customer, who was using a paper handkerchief, to cough in a significant manner, as though warning the speaker.

A DEALER IN BRONZES.

"Those gentlemen are purchasers like yourself," said a shopman, who just then came from the back of the store with a cup of tea. "They are not used to being addressed in that familiar manner."

"Oh!" coolly replied the boy. "I am sure I beg their pardon."

On hearing this the proprietor, an old man who was busily engaged in dusting some vases with a paper flapper, turned, and said,—

"The price of those lanterns is five *yen* (dollars) each."

As he ceased speaking, the building began to shake the bronzes to rattle and fall, and the earth to tremble; wher everybody rose and rushed into the street.

Mrs. Jewett clung to her husband, and Sallie crept close to Johnnie.

The shocks continued for some time, during which the contents of the stores were thrown into heaps, and the tiles came flying off the roofs.

When the vibration ceased, Oto whispered in a scared tone, —

"That was a *jishin* (earthquake)."

"I thought a nitro-glycerine factory had exploded," said Fitz, then, addressing the terror-stricken proprietor, who was regarding his bronzes with a rueful air, he coolly inquired, —

"Five *yen*, did you say? Why, I can buy them in New York for two and a half. How much will you take for them now they have been damaged by the earthquake?"

The old man gazed at him in a bewildered fashion, and murmured, —

"Nothing frightens these foreign gentlemen."

The ladies were really alarmed, and feared a re-occurrence of the shocks, so the Professor decided to return to their lodging, where they found their host in his best garments, preparing to attend a wedding.

"May I accompany you?" said Fitz. "Do you allow foreigners to be present at such ceremonies?"

"I shall be delighted to take you," he said. "Perhaps your father, mother and sister would like to go with us."

"Do people marry just after such a terrible visitation?" asked Sallie, who had not recovered from her scare.

"Yes, we do not mind such trifling shocks as that," replied the man. "Come, it is time we set out."

As the ladies decided to remain at home the Professor stayed with them.

The boys and their friend entered *kago* (litters), and were carried about three miles to a large house in the suburbs of the city.

The screens had been removed from the interior of the dwelling, making a handsome hall, and everything was in readiness for the ceremony.

The visitors were welcomed, then conducted inside the building, and allotted seats on the matted floor.

Upon the wall, in a recess in the centre of the room, hung three *kakemono*, representing *Dai-koku-fuku-jin* (the great black god of wealth), *Fuku-roku-jin* (health-six or longevity god), and a third deity, *Yebisu* (the god of wealth and guardian of markets), who bore a huge carp and carried a lantern. On the *tokonoma* (raised floor of the recess) were a pair of vases in which burnt incense, a miniature rockery and two life-like ivory storks, — emblems of long life.

THE FAITHFUL LOVERS.

A raised tray supported a model of the pine tree of Takasago, at the base of which were tiny figures of the faithful old man and woman, and the fringe-tailed tortoise (emblems of conjugal love and fidelity).

Near this was a smaller tray containing two doves.

A beautiful screen, placed across the far end of the room, concealed the preparations for the simple ceremony.

The dresses of the future bride were exhibited on a rack before the screen, and were objects of great admiration on the part of the guests.

When all was ready, the mother of the bridegroom and his sisters entered, and knelt on the left of the room, the moth... the bride following them, and kneeling on the right.

Then came the happy pair, attended by friends, who, after placing them one on the left and the other on the right of the pine-tree, retired.

A WEDDING CEREMONY.

In a short time two girls, elegantly dressed with their *obi* (girdles) tied in enormous bows, and wearing flowers in their hair, brought in a vessel containing *saké*, and a tray filled with tiny cups.

The ceremony consisted in the young couple and their parents drinking wine. This was repeated until Fitz whispered, —

"I am sure the bride will have a headache."

"Hush," said Johnnie. "The cups do not hold more than a tablespoonful."

The groom, who was dressed in the old *samurai* style (minus the swords), presently rose, bowed, and quitted the apartment, followed by the bride and their relatives.

After a brief interval the servants entered with refreshments, and Mr. Tamai said the ceremony was over.

"Don't they have a *bozu* to marry them?" demanded Fitz, as the boys enjoyed the good things.

"No," answered Oto. "Are all your people married by ministers?"

"I guess not," said Johnnie. "When papa was a justice, he married lots of couples."

"Our marriages are only civil contracts," said Mr. Tamai. "We can divorce our wives whenever we please."

"So can Americans," said Fitz. "You can't beat us at anything, sir."

Their friend smiled, and Oto remarked, —

"Come, boys, your mother is nervous about the earthquake. We will not add to her anxiety. Let us return home."

The boys paid their respects to the bridegroom, who was seated in a recess, smoking with his intimate friends, then quitted the house, entered their *kago*, and were carried swiftly to their destination.

They found Sallie sitting up for them, and eager to learn all about the wedding.

Fitz related what the reader already knows, on hearing which the girl said, —

"Pooh! I am glad I'm not a Japanese! No minister or marriage service, no flowers, no music, no bridesmaids, no wedding tour. I wonder your young ladies ever get married!"

Oto laughed, and merrily replied, —

MONKEY PEAK.

THE VILLAGE OF SOFT WATER.

## CHAPTER IX.

### FROM SHIMONOSEKI TO YOKOHAMA.

> Far away, with its silver cone
> Towering above the mists,
> Stands lordly Fuji-yama,
> The peerless mountain,
> Seen from thirteen provinces. — JAPANESE POEM.

THE Inland Sea, as foreigners term the body of waters lying between the Southern portion of the main Island of Hondo and Shikoku, is full of islands, and the scenery is both romantic and beautiful.

On the morning of the second day out, the ship passed close to a pavilion built upon piers, on a rocky point some distance from the shore, with which it was connected by a wooden bridge.

The architecture of the pavilion, and of a mansion near it, was so different from what the boys had seen in Shimonoseki and Nagasaki, that they commented upon it, when Oto said,—

"Yonder palace was built by the lord of Sanuki in imitation of a similar edifice on the shore of Lake Biwa. A dreadful tragedy once took place in that pavilion."

"Do tell us about it," urged Sallie.

"The story, like most tales of Old Japan, is a sanguinary one," said Oto. "The lord of Sanuki had offended the lord of Awa, and the latter's retainers swore to avenge the insult. One evening, when the owner of that pavilion was entertaining some of his friends, sixty *samurai* (gentry of the clan) of Awa, swam off to the building, and, clambering up the piles, attacked the pleasure-party. The result was a prolonged fight, in which everybody was killed or subsequently died of their ills."

"Jeminy!" ejaculated Fitz. "What was the cause of the quarrel, and why did not the lords fight?"

Oto smiled and answered,—

"It is said that Sanuki contemptuously elevated his nose on passing the lord of Awa. In those days such an act was a deadly insult."

PAVILION OF SANUKI.

"Do you mean to say all that blood was shed because one man turned up his nose at another?" inquired the amazed boy.

"Yes," said Oto. "Revenging such an act was in accordance with *Yamato damashi*, (the spirit of old Japan.) When a great lord was insulted he did not fight his enemy. The *samurai* attended to such little matters."

He told them many stories of a like nature, and, when they were passing Harima, pointed out a turreted structure perched on the rocky shore, which he said was the world-famed castle of Ako, described in the "Loyal Ronins."

"I have read that romance," said Sallie, who just then joined them, and was viewing the scene with intense interest. "I remember the Forty-seven Ronins wanted to die defending the castle, but Sir Big-rock, the chief-councillor, persuaded them to live and to avenge the death of their lord. It is a glorious story."

"I think you were wise to abolish the feudal system," said Johnnie. "You owe America something for awakening your nation from its slumber."

"Yes," said Oto.

"And we owe Japan a million of dollars," said Fitz. "I think the best way will be for us to put that sum to our credit for ending the rule of the great lords."

"We did that ourselves," said Oto. "The arrival of foreigners in our country only hastened what the loyal men of Nihon earnestly desired, the restoration of the Mikado to power. You did not overthrow the Shogunate, our patriots accomplished that."

"All right," coolly answered Fitz. "Then we ought to pay you back that money."

They touched at Kobe and at another port, and stopped at several places in order to discharge and take aboard passengers.

It rained during the remainder of the voyage, and the sky did not clear until the afternoon of the last day of the trip, when the clouds vanished, and they, for the first time, beheld the lofty peak of Fuji-yama.

Although they had seen many representations of the mountain, the sight of it was a surprise, and the scene so impressive that the boys forgot to chatter, and gazed at the snow-capped crest as though fascinated by it.

The cone glistened in the rays of the declining sun, and stood out in bold relief against the pale, rose-tinted sky. The mountain, below the cap, was of a dull, purple color, deepening into black, and the hills in front were of a lovely brown, lighted here and there with gold.

The travellers watched the charming scene until night dropped her mantle, and hid Fuji and its glories from their sight, then they found their tongues, and Mrs. Jewett said, —

"I was prepared to be delighted, still Fuji surpasses my expectations."

"Yes," said the Professor, in a musing tone. "It is the most beautiful mountain in the world. I am not astonished the Japanese artists depict it so frequently, or that the poets are so fond of singing its praises."

"In all the world there is only one Fujiyama," softly quoted Oto.

"It is a grand sight," said Johnnie.

"Perfectly exquisite," murmured Sallie.

"Yes," said Fitz. "What a jolly coast one could have down that slope. I suppose there is lots of ice up there?"

"Of course there is," replied Oto. "Why do you ask?"

"Well, you said that ice was dear in Yokohama," answered the boy. "Now, if you were to build a shoot from the top of Fuji to the bottom, you could send down blocks of ice and supply the Yokohama and Tokio folks with a cheap article."

Oto bit his lips and answered, —

"You always look at the prosaic side of things, Fitz. It would be desecration to build a shoot down the side of Rich-scholar-Peak;" adding, good-humoredly, "you forget that many of my countrymen regard the mountain as holy, and that they perform pilgrimages up its dangerous cone. Nearly every year some one is killed in making the ascent or descent."

"Why not build an inclined railway, then?" said the practical lad. "You might make lots of money taking up pilgrims, and do a carrying-business in ice. You're not a go-ahead people."

"You do not understand what a pilgrimage is," laughingly retorted Oto. "The devout persons who ascend the mountain walk every step, and perform certain ceremonies at each stopping-place. An inclined railway would — would — "

"Convince them that their zeal had been misdirected," said Fitz. "There is nothing like a railway to enlighten people. It brings them face to face with modern science and civilization."

After supper the Jewetts went on deck, and beheld a novel sight.

The bay of Yedo was covered with fishing-boats, each of which carried in its bow a blazing torch, or pan filled with tow and oil.

The lights flared and flickered, the boatmen yelled and shouted hoarsely to one another as they raised their nets from the water, and everything was bustle, noise, and animation.

"They are catching *iwashi* (sardines)" said Oto. "These square nets, suspended from the four corners of the bamboo frames, are often too heavy for the fishermen to raise."

"Why do they burn torches?" asked Sallie. "The moon gives light enough for them to fish by."

"The lights are to attract the fish," answered Oto. "We Japanese are great fish-eaters."

"I thought Buddhists never ate anything that had lived," observed Fitz.

"We are not all Buddhists," replied Oto. "Though two-thirds of our population believe in that faith, many of their number eat fish."

"Is that Yokohama, where the foreign ships are anchored," inquired Mrs. Jewett.

"Yes," said Oto. "As soon as the health-officer has visited us, we shall be allowed to land."

"We intend to remain on board until morning," observed the Professor. "The captain has given us permission to do so."

The "Adzuma" steamed in and out between the fishing-boats, and about ten o'clock dropped anchor off Yokohama. Around her were trading-crafts of all nations, Japanese, American, English, French, and Russian vessels of war, a vast fleet of native coasters, and hundreds of passenger-boats awaiting her arrival. The ship was quickly boarded by the health-officer, who, after having made minute inquiries of the captain, said

FISHING BY TORCH-LIGHT.

the passengers might land, and, stepping to the gangway, hailed the government steam-tug that had brought him, saying, —

"Now you can come aboard."

A crowd of visitors clambered up the vessel's side, and mingling with the passengers, eagerly searched for their friends.

Presently Oto uttered a cry of joy, and rushing toward a grave-looking old gentleman, clad in native garb, threw himself on the deck, and bowed his head; the stranger, who was trembling violently, kneeling and acknowledging the salute.

Similar scenes were enacted all over the ship, though some of the Japanese shook hands in the American fashion.

The Jewetts watched their friend, who said, in a voice choking with emotion, —

"Honorable father, this is indeed a happy moment for me."

"And for me," murmured his parent, down whose cheeks big tears were trickling, and whose hands shook as though he had an ague. "My dear son, I trust you have returned in good health?"

"I am perfectly well," said Oto. "I hope my honorable mother is the same."

"Yes, honorable wife is perfectly healthy," replied the gentleman.

Both of them bowed repeatedly, as they did so, sucking in their breath in a peculiar manner that caused Fitz and Johnnie to smile, and glance significantly at one another.

When the salutations were concluded, Oto rose, and apologizing to the Professor for not having introduced him before, said, —

"I was so overjoyed at once more beholding my father's face that I forgot what was due to you. Honorable father, these are my good friends, Professor and Mrs. Jewett, Miss Sallie, and Johnnie and Fitz, about whom I have so often written you."

Mr. Nambo, who during this speech bowed repeatedly and sucked in his breath more rapidly than before, was about to prostrate himself, and salute the party in Japanese fashion, when the Professor extended his hand and begged he would remain on his feet.

"I am not, like my son, a proficient in your manners," said the agitated old gentleman, grasping the proffered hand. "You must pardon the weakness of a father who has so long been parted from his son. I thank you all, from the bottom of my heart, for the hundred thousand kindnesses you have shown my boy. I hope you will visit our humble home, and be able to content yourselves with the miserable accommodation I can offer." Then he turned to Oto and said: "Your mother has repeated many prayers for your safe return. Buddha has answered them. You will have to make a special offering to Kuwannon and Benten for their merciful goodness to you."

The irrepressible Fitz, hearing this speech, whispered to Oto, in English,—

"You'll have to hang a pair of your old gum-boots in the temple, see if you won't."

"Hush!" said his mother, frowning.

Mr. Nambo, who had not understood this, renewed his bows, sucked in his breath, and said,—

"My son, a number of your college friends have come with me to welcome you back to your native land. Will you see them?"

"Of course," replied the delighted youth. "I feel just crazy to say, 'how do you do?' to the boys."

In a few moments a crowd of young men dressed in American costume, came rushing along the deck. After being introduced to the strangers, they shook hands with Oto, in foreign style, and welcomed him in English.

"Hai, old fellow!" cried one. "Why, you look just splendid."

"You have brought home a lot of new ideas, I suppose," said another, who wore spectacles. "We are waiting for you to join our class. The college has been rebuilt, and we are turning out M. D's as fast as the Harvard Medical School."

They had with them the materials for a feast, which they

quickly spread up⸺ ⸺k; and amid much merriment the Jewetts joined in ⸺ ⸺r to Oto's return.

The captain and officers looked on, and enjoyed the s⸺ as much as any one.

In the midst of the excitement, a steam-tug came alongside, and they heard a cheery voice shouting, in English,—

"Adzuma, ahoy! Have you any passengers on board named Jewett?"

Up sprang the Professor, Johnnie and Fitz, and soon a tall gentleman clambered over the gangway, and advancing to them, held out his hands, saying,—

"I suppose you are my brother John and his sons?"

A happy time followed, Mrs. Jewett and Sallie being introduced to their relation whom they had never seen; Dr. Jewett having resided in Japan over twenty years.

He welcomed Oto warmly, and with his relatives joined the group, and partook of the feast, which consisted of cakes, wine, and all manner of Japanese delicacies.

They sat up till nearly midnight, when Mrs. Jewett said,—

"Come, Sallie, we must retire. Good-night, gentlemen, this has indeed been a pleasant evening."

Mr. Nambo, Oto, and his college chums smoked and chatted long after their American friends had retired, and did not seek repose until the day was beginning to dawn.

## CHAPTER X.

### YOKOHAMA.

> Where formerly the traveller beheld only a few huts
> Inhabited by poor fishermen,
> And a temple dedicated to Benten,
> He now sees a wealthy city,
> Half foreign, half native.
> This place is called Yokohama. — JAPANESE POEM.

EARLY the next morning, the party embarked in boats, and were landed on the small *hatoba* (stone pier of Yokohama), where they found a carriage waiting to convey them to the Bluff; a high, wooded promontory, on the left of the Bund or business part of the city.

Yokohama is built on a little island, separated from the mainland by a narrow river, crossed by several bridges, and is neatly paved and lighted by gas from works owned by a native gentleman named Takashimaya.

Dr. Jewett had many friends in the place, and one of his intimates, an American merchant named Massey, had invited the travellers to stay at his residence.

Sallie mounted her pony, and the rest of the party entered the vehicle, which was driven by a native coachman, clad in English livery.

As the visitors proceeded through the streets they saw many first-class dry-goods stores, confectioner's stores, photograph-galleries, eating-houses, jewellers' shops, and newspaper offices.

"Why, it is like home," said Fitz. "Jeminy! there's a dentist's. I can have my teeth attended to."

YOKOHAMA FROM THE BLUFF.

The carriage was driven in and out among a moving crowd of similar vehicles, nearly all the merchants owning conveyances drawn by horses. The new-comers also noticed hundreds of *jin-riki-sha*, propelled by hardy-looking runners, who shouted vociferously, and appeared to enjoy the exercise.

The police were in uniform, and everything denoted a well-regulated city, the inhabitants of which were doing a prosperous business.

After a pleasant ride, the party arrived at the residence of Dr. Jewett's friend, who, with his wife, welcomed them to Yokohama, and made them feel perfectly at home.

When they had enjoyed the luxury of a bath and had breakfasted, they sat in the veranda, looked down upon the settlement, and spied through a telescope at the vessels riding at anchor in the bay of Yedo.

The houses were mostly of brick or stone, and were built entirely by Japanese artisans.

About ten o'clock, Johnnie and Fitz started for a walk, leaving their parents and Sallie to enjoy the society of their host and hostess. Dr. Jewett, Oto, and his father had gone to Tokio, so the brothers were left to their own resources.

"Yokohama means across the beach," said Johnnie. "They ought to have called it Swamptown. Most of the new houses are built in a puddle."

"I guess they, like the Bostonians, have used up all the dry land, and are taking to the mud," laughingly replied Fitz, as they halted before a building which some plasterers were covering with stucco. "See how differently the Japanese do things from us. Instead of using hods, they scoop up the stucco with long shovels, which they raise to the stages occupied by the plasterers."

"Yes, and most of them squat at their work," said Johnnie.

"What a strangely-shaped tool that carpenter is using,"

remarked his brother. "It is made like a hoe. I suppose those young men in long *kimono* (coats) are the foremen. What can their sticks be for?"

"Those are measuring-rods," answered the other. "See, one of them has a builder's square in his hand."

JAPANESE BUILDERS AT WORK.

They watched the busy scene, and chatted with the superintendents, who informed the boys that they had been in America, and had worked on the New York Elevated Railroad.

While they were talking, a lad passed, carrying a big, ugly poodle.

"Why don't you let that dog walk?" inquired Fitz.

The bearer grinned and, halting, replied, —

"This is a very valuable animal, and I have strict orders not to lose him."

"Is that why you carry him?" inquired the amused American.

The boy nodded, and said,—

A FOREIGN DOG AND ITS ATTENDANT.

"Yes—partly. You see, if he gets muddy I have to wash him, which he does not like; so I prefer to carry him like a child."

"Why not tie a string to his collar?" said Johnnie.

"Didn't I tell you he would get muddy?" returned the dog carrier. "You are an American, are you not?"

"What makes you think that?" demanded Fitz.

"Because you ask a hundred thousand questions," was the saucy response. "I once lived with an American, but he was too smart, and wouldn't let me make my little perquisites. I like the English; they are more easily pleased than your people."

Away he went, leaving the brothers laughing at his impudent manner.

"He has lived with the English, and learned to be cheeky," remarked one of the builders. "Our boys are not all like him."

"I think he is real smart," said Johnnie. "What right had we to bother him with our questions?"

The young Americans bade the builders *sayonara* (adieu, or farewell) then strolled through the Bund, or business portion of the foreign settlement, which was well-paved, and had concrete sidewalks.

"The warehouses are like our own," said Fitz.

"Yes," nodded Johnnie. "I guess the merchants are mostly American or English. Suppose we go on to the Japanese quarter."

"What a number of Chinamen there are here," observed his brother, as they watched a neatly dressed clerk, who was giving a Japanese coolie instructions about the conveyance of some bales of goods. "How fat and well-to-do they look."

His speech was overheard by the man, and when they had passed he said to the coolie, —

A CHINESE CLERK.

"Those are Americans. Never go to their country, they treat foreigners like dogs."

Fitz was about to reply, but Johnnie said, —

"Hush, brother, you had no right to make the remark, besides, he only spoke the truth."

They met coolies carrying immense loads of empty cases, and watched a man varnishing the outside of some tea-chests, and a native merchant weighing tea with wooden balances.

"Why do you put that stuff on the chests?" inquired Johnnie.

"To make them waterproof," answered the workman. "The sea-air penetrates into the holds of the ships, and, if it were not for the lead cases and this varnish, would spoil the tea. Your honorable countrymen are our best customers."

"Do you like the Chinese?" demanded Fitz.

The coolie glanced at his interrogator and answered,—

"Not — particularly."

"Why not?"

"They are too smart," returned the man. "I wish they would not come here and gobble up all the best situations."

"Why do you not supplant them?" said Johnnie.

The man scratched his ear, and thought awhile, then said,—

"They are too much for us. Can *you* get rid of them after they have once settled in your honorable country?"

"I do not think we can," answered Fitz.

The coolie laughed bitterly and said, in a sing-song tone:

> "You can kill a fly and
> Smoke out a mosquito,
> But you cannot dislodge a Chinaman!
> They do not conquer a country
> By force of arms, but
> By dint of patience and numbers."

"That is a clever satire!" said Johnnie. "Who composed it?"

"I read it in yesterday's paper," was the answer.

"Do you have dailies?" inquired Fitz.

"Yes, we have also many weekly newspapers. My brother, who is a wealthy man, edits one."

"Then why are you not in his employ?"

"I am too fond of *saké* (rice wine)," was the candid response. "If I were not, I should be better off. *Sayonara.*"

In the Japanese quarter of Yokohama the brothers saw many large stores filled with works of art.

"Want anything to buy?" asked one of the dealers in

A CURIO STORE.

broken English. "Everything what you want, got here — yees!"

"How much for that large cabinet?" asked Fitz.

He spoke in English, so the man, not imagining the boys understood Japanese, said to his employer, —

"How much am I to ask these innocent foreigners for that?"

"Five hundred dollars," replied the proprietor.

When this was translated, they pretended to be anxious to purchase, and putting off their shoes, stepped over the shop-board and began to examine the wares.

"Ask them four hundred," presently observed the proprietor. "They will give any sum for an article they fancy."

"We do not want to pay foreign prices," said Johnnie in Japanese. "We could get a cabinet like that cheaper in New York."

The amazed dealers bowed, and when his man had offered the customers tea, the master said, —

"Evidently you know the real value of things. Just say what you will give and I will accept or reject your offer."

"Is that your way of doing business?" asked Fitz.

"Yes, with honorable foreigners who can speak our language," was the prompt reply.

They purchased some *hashi* (chopsticks), and inquired of the men whether there was anything to be seen in Yokohama.

"Have you been to the temple of Benten?" said the dealer.

"No."

"Go there, you will find it at the end of Benten tori (street). It is well worth seeing."

The brothers quitted the store, and after walking down an avenue, saw a weather-beaten *torii*, denoting the entrance to the temple.

It had a forlorn look, and the surroundings were in keeping

with the appearance of the structure. Beyond it was a second *torii* and two stone lanterns, then a number of dilapidated buildings and a grove, in which stood the temple of Ben-zai-tin-njo, or Benten, the goddess of the sea.

The lads ascended the steps of the building and putting off their shoes, entered the main portion in which was a shrine

THE BENTEN TORI (AVENUE) AND TORII.

containing the image of the goddess, who was represented as sitting on a rock overlooking the waves and playing on a *biwa* (pear-shaped guitar).

Below her, in the surf, was a black object, which a ragged mendicant, who spoke horrible English, and who took charge of the foreign strangers, informed them was intended to represent a dragon.

Their self-appointed guide proved to be a thorough nuisance, so Fitz said, in Japanese, to a young *bozu*, who was dusting an idol, —

"Is this one of your people?"

The *bozu* ordered the man to be off, whereupon the fellow departed, muttering: "Yeh! those foreigners are mean, they have learned our language in order to deprive us poor guides and interpreters of our living. I wonder how they would like us to go to their country and learn their — gibberish?"

THE GODDESS BENTEN.

The young *bozu* proved to be a very pleasant, gentle person, and was most kind and attentive to his visitors, showing them the various objects of interest, and explaining everything that puzzled them.

On the left of the main altar was a recess filled with rude models of native craft, some large and the others mere toys.

"Those were deposited there by persons whom Benten has delivered from shipwreck," said their guide. "Ah! if people would only have more faith in her."

"Who was Benten?" asked Fitz.

"Have you never heard?" queried the young *bozu*. "Come with me up in the roof, where it is cool, and I will tell you all about our wonderful goddess."

They ascended a number of dusty ladders, and presently found themselves on a platform of rough boards, placed across the beams, between the first and second roofs of the structure.

Below them, like a panorama, was Yokohama and the Bay of Yedo, and away in the distance they beheld the blue mountains of Awa and Kadzusa.

"I am not on duty now," said the *bozu*; "I thought if we came up here we would have an opportunity to talk without being disturbed by these wretched beggars."

He produced a pipe, some finely-cut tobacco, and a flint and steel, which he politely offered to his guests.

"Thank you, we do not smoke," said Johnnie.

"I am not supposed to," said their new friend, in an apologetical manner, "but I am sometimes tempted to do it, I am so lonely."

"Oh, go ahead," answered Johnnie. "Enjoy yourself while you can, we won't tell any one."

The *bozu* filled the tiny bowl of his pipe, and after taking a few puffs, knocked out the ashes, and said,—

"I promised to enlighten you about Benten. Many centuries ago, when this part of Japan was very swampy—"

"It is pretty soft round here now," murmured Fitz, glancing down upon the settlement.

"You are right," said their entertainer. "But in those days it was much worse, and the land was infested with dragons;" pausing, and refilling his pipe. "Have you any of those monsters in your honorable country?"

"No," said Fitz; "though we can beat the world in the matter of alligators. We make boots out of their skins."

This reply puzzled the *bozu*, who scratched his ear, and continued,—

"Those dragons played havoc with the people, sometimes devouring a hundred children every day. Of course no country could stand such a drain on its population. Strange to say, the creatures seldom killed adults or aged persons."

"Guess the latter were too tough," suggested Fitz.

The *bozu* did not smile, but went on,—

"They used to fight and tear up the ground, and the air was filled with their roars and cries, which caused the people to quake with fear and pray to the gods. One night, when the monsters were having a desperate battle in the marshes, a storm arose and stopped them. At dawn, when it cleared off, Benten was seen in a cloud-rift, and the fishermen heard sounds of celestial music. As she revealed herself, the dragons vanished, and the island of Enoshima rose from the waters of the bay. Having conferred this blessing on mankind, she retired to her abode beneath the waves. Whenever it storms we pray to her, and upon moonlight nights she is often seen on the edge of the cliffs, sitting with her *biwa* on her knees, and playing most ravishing airs. At her command, the winds blow and the waters rise and fall. She had a large family, and is worshipped as a model mother and housekeeper;" adding, as he once more filled his pipe: "I could talk forever about Benten."

"What is that building down there, close to your rear gate?" asked Johnnie.

"Another church," replied the *bozu*, with a sigh. "You foreigners are ruining our temples. When I came here we had a larger number of worshippers than the building could accommodate; now we only see a few old women who put brass cash in the money-box. Why do your missionaries not stay at home and convert your sailors and merchants? they need it badly enough."

Then he again sighed, and gazed ruefully at the walls of the new church.

"Guess you are run down," said Fitz. "Don't you ever take a vacation?"

"No; I cannot leave my superior, who is a very old man. My only amusement is to sit up here and smoke. I often cry for hours together. What do you do when you feel sad?"

"Ask mother to give me some medicine," said Fitz.

"If I only had something to distract my attention, I should be happy," said the poor fellow. "Cannot you tell me of anything that would help me to pass the time; I mean a problem to work out. We *bozu* have invented many different ones, but I know them all. Have you Americans any such things?"

Fitz glanced slyly at his brother, and said,—

"I suppose you have heard of the *jiugo-ban komaraseru* (fifteen puzzle)?"

"Do you refer to the fifteen visions of Benten?"

"No; it is a simple cure for such a complaint as yours," answered Fitz. "It was invented by an American."

He took a piece of paper from his pocket-book, and cutting it into squares, marked each with a Japanese number. The *bozu* watched the proceedings with the greatest interest, and asked a hundred questions, his childlike manner greatly amusing the boys.

Fitz arranged the papers, and explained how they were to be moved, when the young man said,—

"I must show this to my superior. Come, he will be glad to see you. Any visitor is welcome here nowadays."

They descended to the floor of the temple, and entering a small room behind the centre altar, beheld a very old man, who had in his hands a brush of long, white horse-hair, mounted on an ivory handle. He was very deaf, and had not a tooth in his head.

The young *bozu* shouted into his ear, and exhibited the puzzle, on seeing which the old man mumbled, —

"I know this. It was invented by Jimmu Tenno, and no person has ever solved it."

"Who was Jimmu Tenno?" shouted Fitz.

The old gentleman waved his horse-tail, and relapsing into a sort of doze, mumbled, —

"*Nammiyo! Nammiyo!*"

"What does he mean?" demanded the inquisitive boy.

"He is praying," whispered the young *bozu*. "Jimmu Tenno was our first Mikado (Emperor). That puzzle is twenty-five hundred years old. There is nothing new in the world."

"Did not Jimmu Tenno also discover electricity, and invent the steam-engine and telephone?" asked Johnnie.

"No," gravely answered the *bozu*. "He was not a magician. Those things were the inventions of evil demons."

While they were conversing, the old man continued to mumble; so Fitz said to their friend, —

"Why does he say *Nammiyo?*"

"To save the trouble of repeating the entire prayer," gravely replied the *bozu*. "We take *na* from the first word, *mi* from the second, and *yo* from the sound of *Butsu*. It saves time."

The boys smiled.

"Say," said Fitz, "why does he wave that horse-tail so? To keep off the flies?"

"That is a sacred emblem, and denotes authority," returned the *bozu*. "We regard it as you do the sceptre of your king."

"King!" cried Fitz. "We have no kings in our country. We rule ourselves."

The young man regarded them with astonishment, then murmured, as though thinking aloud, —

"How can a nation exist that does not believe in Benten, and has no head?"

"Oh! we get along well enough with a President," bluntly answered Fitz.

Their guide then led the way into a grove of bamboo, in the rear of the temple, and, pointing to some tombs, said, —

"This is our burial-ground. Is it not a delightful spot to sit and think in?"

"I'm not particularly partial to cemeteries," said Johnnie. "I wonder you don't move those tombs and sell the land for building purposes. Who is this man coming towards us?"

"He is a beggar *bozu*," was the contemptuous reply. "They are a nuisance. We are poor enough without being compelled to share our rice with them."

The stranger approached, and, bowing to the boys, said, —

"Honorable sirs, there is a telegraph messenger looking for you. He has followed you from the Bluff."

It sounded comical to hear such a speech from a shaven-headed *bozu*, and the boys could not refrain from smiling.

"Bring the messenger hither," said their friend.

The stranger retired, and soon returned with a lad clothed in the uniform of the telegraph company, who, after inquiring whether the Americans were named Jewett, handed them an envelope, saying, —

"Twenty *sen*. Please pay me, and sign my book."

While Fitz was doing this, his brother read the telegram, which was dated Tokio, and ran as follows, —

"Tell your father that I shall come to Yokohama early to-morrow. Everything is ready for your reception here. — OTO."

The boys bade the young *bozu* adieu, and, as they quitted the grounds, saw him squatting near one of the tombs working out his puzzle.

"What a strange country this is!" said Johnnie. "Benten, the telegraph; ancient superstitions and modern civilization jostling one another and struggling for the mastery."

"The telegraph will wipe Benten out of existence," said Fitz. "That *bozu* let the cat out of the bag when he said our modern discoveries were the inventions of demons. Benten will have to take her banjo and retire to her watery domain. She cannot conjure the dragons called steam, electricity, and the printing-press; nor can her *bozu* — "

"Solve the ancient fifteen puzzle," added Johnnie.

They laughed and chatted as they walked to the Bluff, on reaching which they met their parents and Sallie, out for a drive.

Johnnie showed them the telegram, when the Professor said, —

"Your uncle has the refusal of a house for us, and has obtained permission for us to travel anywhere for six months. We will first visit Oto's relations, then take up our residence in our new abode, which is in the hilly part of the city of Tokio."

"Boys," inquired Mrs. Jewett, "what have you been doing with yourselves this morning?"

The boys laughed, and said, —

"We have been making the acquaintance of Mrs. Benten, and instructing one of her servants in the fifteen puzzle."

The Professor was highly amused with his son's account of their adventures, and remarked, —

"You are right, Johnnie. In a few years the temples will be emptied of their rubbish, and —"

"Turned into telegraph offices," suggested Fitz. "Good-bye, sir. You continue your drive; we are going to the dentist's."

## CHAPTER XI.

### TOKIO.

*When Yamato Daké arrived at Sakamoto
He gazed down upon the plain and bay of Yedo,
And remembering his beloved Tachibana-hime,
Cried, "Adzuma! Adzuma!" (my wife, my wife.)*
JAPANESE POEM.

TOKIO (the Eastern Capital), formerly called Yedo, is eighteen miles from Yokohama, and is connected with the settlement by a well-kept railway that has a double track, iron bridges, and handsome dêpôts.

Oto arrived, according to promise, and at noon the travellers quitted their friends on the Bluff, and drove to the Yokohama terminus; a stone building, in which were a crowd of Japanese waiting for the train to start.

Nearly all of them were dressed in native costume, and wore high clogs of wood that rattled on the floor in a very noisy manner.

"Chinese everywhere," said Fitz, as his father changed some gold into *kinsato* (paper money). "Japan will be ruined by cheap Chinese labor."

"All our porters and dépôt-masters are Japanese," quickly retorted Oto. "Many of your railway officials are of foreign birth."

"Your conductors and engine-drivers are not natives," answered the boy; "they are our countrymen."

"Wrong for once," said Oto quietly. "They are Englishmen. We contracted to employ the men for a certain number of years, and are obliged to keep them on, or break our word.

As soon as their time is up, we have natives fully competent to take their places."

The fare for each person was a *yen*, and baggage was charged extra, but not checked, as in the States.

A *betto* (groom) had been hired to ride Abraham Lincoln to Tokio, and two of Mr. Nambo's servants sent down to take Mrs. Jewett's *jin-riki-sha* by road.

The Doctor was at the hospital in Tokio, but his popularity was felt by his relatives, who were treated with great kindness by the railway employés.

"Anything for the friends of the good Doctor," said the conductor. "When I was sick last year, he was ever so kind to me."

The tickets were marked from "Yokohama to Shinbashi," a village once distant from the capital, though now forming part of its suburbs.

The train quitted the charming environs of Yokohama, entered the plain of Yedo, rattled along the shore of the bay, and crossed several streams, on one of which Fitz spied a basket moored by a line.

"I don't believe you can guess the use of that apparatus," said Oto.

"It is a fish-trap," said the boy.

"A lobster-pot," suggested Johnnie.

"An old basket, thrown away as useless," said Sallie.

"No," was the smiling reply. "It is a duckling protector. The water-rats, hereabouts, are so numerous that the country folks are obliged to put their young ducks in such contrivances. It has one end higher than the other, and is made of strong bamboo, bound with iron hoops."

"Sold!" cried Fitz. "We don't want such machines in our country. We raise our ducks by steam!"

After a pleasant ride they reached their destination, where

they found hundreds of *jin-riki-sha* waiting to convey the passengers to any part of the city.

Each of the travellers engaged a vehicle, and when all were seated, they started for Oto's home.

A *jin-riki-sha* is only a large baby-carriage, with shafts like a cart, and is drawn by one or more men. In Tokio nearly all of them have two attendants, one to run in the shafts, and the other to pull on a rope or push behind. These coolies wear decent dresses, are licensed, and have their heads partly shaven in the old style.

The travellers, after going a long distance through narrow streets and over many canals, were trundled over the world-famed Nippon Bashi (great bridge of Japan), from which they caught a passing glimpse of Fuji-yama.

The bridge, a wooden structure much inferior to many others in the city, was thronged with people, and the noise of their clogs, the rumbling of the carts and other vehicles, and shouts of the *jin-riki-sha* men were almost deafening.

Coolies, carrying enormous fish suspended from bamboo poles, were running to and fro; the bridge being in the vicinity of the largest market in the city, and the landing-place for fishermen, who arrived with their finny prizes at all hours of the day.

The boys had been told that all distances in Japan were measured from the Nippon Bashi, so Fitz shouted to Oto,—

" Say, where is the first mile-stone? "

" A mile from here, in any direction," was the laughing answer.

On they went through streets filled with shops and alive with pedestrians.

Nearly every person wore the national dress; only aliens, officials, soldiers, sailors, policemen, and a few mercnants and students being clothed in foreign garb.

The ladies were neatly attired, and nobody was without garments.

The *jin-riki-sha* men spun their vehicles along at a rapid pace, and presently entered an avenue lined with long buildings that were pierced at intervals with small windows, and

THE GATEWAY OF MR. NAMBO'S ESTABLISHMENT.

separated from the roadway by deep ditches containing running water.

"Which is your *yashiki* (mansion)?" inquired Oto's coolie.

The young man pointed ahead, to a narrow gateway between two of the barrack-like structures, and said, —

"That is my honorable father's. He is on the watch for us."

The avenue was broad, and the houses and fences in excellent repair. Beyond, on a little hill, was a lovely park filled with beautiful trees.

A few persons only were to be seen, and the place wore an air of repose and respectability. When the *jin-riki-sha* stopped in front of the gateway, Mr. Nambo advanced, and assisted the ladies to alight, saying,—

"I fear you have had a most wearisome ride. Welcome to my miserable abode, which is not worthy to be honored by your august presence."

He sucked in his breath in a (Japanese) gentlemanly manner, then, after bowing repeatedly, conducted his guests across the narrow bridge, through the gateway, and into a garden filled with glorious flowers, variegated shrubs, and noble trees. In the midst of this earthly paradise stood a number of beautifully decorated buildings that denoted both the wealth and good taste of their owner.

"What a charming spot!" exclaimed Mrs. Jewett.

"Any monkeys in those trees?" demanded Fitz.

"No," smilingly replied Oto; "but we have lots of foxes in our grounds."

"There is my wife by the house," said Mr. Nambo. "My niece is sitting near her."

On hearing his voice, the younger lady rose and advanced with her aunt to greet their visitors.

When Mr. Nambo presented his wife, she shook hands with Mrs. Jewett and Sallie, and bowing to the Professor and boys, said, in a voice choking with emotion,—

"How can I thank you for all your kindness to our dear son? I little thought, when he was sent to your honorable country, he would find a second mother and father."

"Oto brought his own recommendation, and we could not help liking him," replied the lady. "We all think everything of him."

They were then introduced to the niece, O-Kiku (Miss Chrysanthemum), who, to their astonishment, spoke excellent English.

"I was educated in the Ladies' College," she said. "I have come to keep Miss Sallie company."

O-KIKU (MISS CHRYSANTHEMUM).

"Yes," gently added Oto's mother, who, spite of her shaven eyebrows, blackened teeth, and wrinkles, was a charming lady; "we thought your daughter would like a companion of her own age."

MR. NAMBO'S HOME.

After chatting a while, they entered the first house on their left, which was arranged and furnished in foreign style.

"We hope you will not think of taking up your abode in the Northern district," observed Mr. Nambo. "It is a very unhealthy locality, and you will be devoured by mosquitos. We have always expected the honor of entertaining you, and shall feel grieved if you do not stay with us."

There was no resisting such a pressing invitation, so the Professor accepted it.

"This is the American part of our establishment," said Mrs. Nambo, as the party seated themselves and partook of tea, served by a light-footed maid. "We furnished it years ago for Oto and his friends. Though I did not like him to wear foreign clothes, I made no objection to his sleeping on a bed, and having chairs and tables in his rooms."

The visitors laughed, and Mrs. Jewett related how she had stripped Oto's chamber to make him feel at home.

On hearing the story, Miss Chrysanthemum, who was seated on a chair in the veranda, and who still retained her clogs, laughingly remarked, —

"Well, I should smile! You don't tell me! Cousin Oto used to sleep on an American bed at the Imperial College."

"Yes; and a shocking hard one it was," said Oto. "At first, before the faculty learned the arrangement of foreign beds, we had no mattresses; and were compelled to lie upon mat-covered boards, placed on the hard slats of the bedsteads."

"That is nothing," said his cousin. "When an English friend presented my honorable father with a brass bedstead, we thought it was a frame to train plants on, and placed it in the garden. I guess some of our articles puzzle foreigners as greatly as that did us!"

She laughed so merrily, and was so good-tempered and nice, that the visitors liked her at once.

"Where did you learn to say, 'Well, I should smile'?" asked Fitz, taking a seat on the veranda near her.

"Of my teacher," she replied. "Isn't it correct?"

"It is not considered quite genteel," said Oto, joining them. "Of course, people use that expression, but it is better to say: 'You surprise me,' or 'That is very amusing.'"

The young lady bit her lips, and murmured, —

"Oh, bother!"

When the visitors had rested they were conducted to their respective rooms. Mrs. Nambo accompanied the ladies, and Oto showed the boys their quarters.

The apartments were not screened as in an ordinary Japanese house, but divided by walls, which were covered with stamped paper that looked like leather.

In the rear of Mrs. Jewett's room was a miniature garden, representing a lake crossed by a bridge, the approaches to which were guarded with gates.

"I arranged that from a picture of a view in your Central Park, sent me by Oto," said the hostess. "I wanted you to imagine you were looking at a scene in your honorable country. Have I modelled the gates correctly?"

"Beautifully," answered Mrs. Jewett. "I feel quite at home. Are there any frogs in that pond?"

"No; it is filled with tame gold-fish. You will find them quite amusing, and they don't stray about a house as frogs do. If you ring that bell, they will swim up to the landing for their food. They were Oto's pets, so I have kept them for him. Ah! he is a good boy!"

After they had chatted about various matters, Mrs. Jewett inquired what the lady thought of her son's change of opinions.

Mrs. Nambo hesitated for a moment, then said, —

"Oto has arrived at years of discretion, and knows his own

mind. He has told me what he believes, and I am endeavoring to bear it without murmuring. Still — I am deeply grieved." She wept softly for awhile, then added: "It is harder to bear than was our long separation. I suppose he knows best, and that we are all wrong."

Mrs. Jewett, finding the subject a painful one, changed the conversation, and spoke of her pleasant experiences in Southern Japan.

While the ladies were conversing, Oto and the boys were talking in the latter's room.

"Say," said Fitz, "your father spoke of his humble abode, so we expected to find a very different place from this."

"We never boast of our belongings," replied their friend. "My father is tolerably wealthy, though not so rich as formerly. This estate once belonged to our *daimio*. My parent bought it of the Government. It is quite an extensive place."

He drew aside a curtain, and revealed a beautiful gateway with heavy doors, on which sky-dogs and *mon* (crests) were carved in bold relief.

"How came the courtyard in such a dilapidated state?" demanded Johnnie.

"This was once the main entrance to the *yashiki* (mansion)," replied Oto. "The low wall and yonder ruined stone lantern were part of a temple destroyed during the war. My father tore down the remains of the structure, and built this house for me. My education and the many demands upon his purse have prevented him from carrying out his original plan."

"What was that?" asked Fitz.

"To rebuild the temple," slyly answered Oto. "Now, I shall have the rubbish cleared away, and mean to erect a laboratory on the spot."

"What does that man, who is sitting there, want of us?" said Johnnie.

RUINS OF A GATEWAY.

"He is the *betto* (groom) who rode your sister's pony from Yokohama," returned Oto. "He desires to know if you will engage him. Now you have agreed to be our guests, you will not require his services. We have plenty of help, and the pony will be well cared for."

The boys gave the groom a dollar, and he went away happy.

"Now come and see my room," said their friend.

They followed him into the next apartment, where they saw a large library, a neat bed above which hung a mosquito netting, lounges, chairs, tables, and a fireplace for burning wood.

"A few years ago this house was the only one in Tokio with a chimney," remarked Oto. "Father was thought crazy for building it, but now many dwellings are fitted with such conveniences."

"What do your people do in winter?" said Johnnie.

"They put on plenty of clothing, and shiver over the *hibachi* (fire-bowl). We are far behind you in the matter of warming our houses."

Next to Oto's room was a small room furnished in Japanese style.

"My foster-mother lives in there," whispered Oto. "Come and say something kind to her. She is greatly grieved at my having become so Americanized."

Fitz and Johnnie followed him, and beheld two women, the elder of whom was boiling water over a charcoal fire enclosed in a box.

Behind her was a metal mirror resting on a frame, and near her companion was a *samisen*, some cups, and a bottle.

On seeing the visitors, both women prostrated themselves, and knocked their foreheads on the matted floor.

"These are my good friends, Johnnie and Fitz," said Oto.

"Come, Mitsu-ro (Mrs. Beeswax), they wish to speak with you."

"Beeswax," murmured Fitz, smiling. "What a comical name for a woman."

Oto made a gesture of reproof, and when the old lady sat up, said,—

"This is Johnnie Sama (Mr.), and this is Fitz Sama."

OTO'S FOSTER-MOTHER.

"I thank you for being kind to my honorable foster-son," said the melancholy-featured dame. "Why did you bewitch him and blind him to the truth?"

"Don't mind what she says," whispered Oto, in English. "Say something complimentary to her."

This puzzled his companions.

"Why does the other one stay doubled up in that fashion?" asked Fitz, in English, indicating the daughter, who remained in the respectful attitude.

"Say something complimentary to my nurse," urged Oto.

"Anything will do. You surely can recollect a short poem? Our old servants are always pleased with such things."

"Jeminy!" murmured Fitz. "Poem — oh, I know! Honorable aged lady," addressing her in Japanese, and bowing in the correct native style: "*Také ni suzumé wa shinayoku tomaru Tometé tomarunu irono michi.*"

On hearing this the dame giggled, and the daughter crammed her sleeve in her mouth, to keep from laughing outright.

Fitz had repeated a sentimental poem, which is thus translated:

> "Though the sparrow can find a resting-place
> On the slender spray of the bamboo,
> Alas! I can find no resting-place
> Near thee."

"That will do splendidly," said Oto. "Now, Mitsuro, say something in return."

The amused old woman assumed a grave air, and folding her hands, murmured, —

"*Tsuru wa sennen.*" (The stork lives a thousand years — meaning, may you, like the stork, live a long life.)

"Won't you pay her a compliment, Johnnie," whispered Oto.

"I think Fitz has said enough," was the cautious reply. "I am not a good hand at speaking pieces."

They drank a cup of tea and ate a few sweetmeats; then retired.

After that the old lady took charge of them, and treated the young Americans as she did Oto.

Japanese servants almost worship their masters, and are permitted to do and say many things that would astonish our domestics.

"Why does she live near you?" asked Fitz, as they returned to Oto's room.

"She was my foster-mother, and has always occupied a room adjoining mine," he said. "When I was in the States she took charge of my quarters and kept them ready for my return. If I cough in the night, she comes in to give me medicine, and is very good to me."

"She won't want to dose us, will she?" inquired Johnnie.

"Don't worry yourself," was the laughing rejoinder. "She has the rheumatism and cannot walk very far. These old servants are very dear to us, and you must make allowances for their peculiarities."

"Why did she laugh at my poem?" demanded Fitz.

Oto chuckled and said, —

"We do not repeat such a verse to aged persons."

"I thought you said any poem would do. You know you wrote that in the book you sent home one New Year."

"Yes," nodded Oto; "but that was to my cousin. We do not compare old women to pretty little sparrows, and express a wish to find a resting-place near them."

"Phewgh!" ejaculated the boy. "You have been making fun of me. Do you call that treating a stranger hospitably?"

"It is not so bad as our firing cucumbers at Oto," said his brother. "I think it is a capital joke."

"You don't catch Fitz Jewett quoting poems any more," he growled. "Though it may be a Japanese fashion, I won't adopt it. Mrs. Beeswax will have many a laugh at my expense."

The boys were summoned to a late dinner, served in a fashion termed *san-no-zen* (three tables), from the fact of each guest being provided with that number of *zen*. This is considered a mark of great respect to visitors and friends, and is only used on extraordinary occasions.

The meal consisted of three courses, at each of which soup was served. The solids comprised broiled and boiled fish, raw carp, cut into thread-like shreds, various kinds of vegetables and pickles, and a dish composed of boiled quail, cut into cubes and smothered in a yellowish sauce.

Each table contained eight or ten bowls of food, and the delicacies were thoroughly cooked and daintily served.

Every one ate with chopsticks and heartily enjoyed the meal.

Tea, rice, and wine were served with each course, and the attendants came and went like waiters at a restaurant.

When the repast was over, Mr. Nambo conducted the guests into his study, a handsomely decorated room, containing many choice *kakemono* (hanging pictures) and some oil-paintings.

THE INDIGNANT NOBLE.

"What is that old gentleman supposed to be doing?" asked Fitz, pointing to a picture representing a noble, in flowing robes and curiously shaped head-dress, belaboring another of his rank with a paper pillow.

"That is a most interesting story," replied Mr. Nambo. "Years ago there lived in Ize a noble who was a great purist, and would never permit any one to use vulgar or incorrect words in his presence. One day, a young noble was sent to inform him that he was shortly to be advanced in rank. In making the announcement the messenger pronounced the word advance in a manner that might either be understood to mean promotion or punishment, whereupon the purist seized his pillow, and grasping the offender by the back of the neck, forced him to the floor, and beat him severely, crying: 'I am to be punished, am I? Take that! In future you will know better than to assassinate our honorable language.'"

"He could not understand a joke," said Fitz.

"Our teachers reverence his memory," observed Mr. Nambo. "We do not approve of taking liberties with time-honored words. I think he did quite right. What do you say, Johnnie Sama?"

Johnnie eyed the picture, and replied in a musing tone,—

"If I had been the messenger, I would have sued him for assault and battery and got heavy damages. I think he must have been crazy. If we punished people for making puns, our prisons would be full."

"John!" sternly ejaculated his father.

"It is true, sir," was the innocent reply. "You have told us so lots of times."

The Professor pursed his lips, and turning to an oil-painting representing two murderous-looking individuals, waiting, sword in hand, in a dark corner, asked,—

"Pray, who were those?"

"Ah!" smilingly answered their host, sucking in his breath, "that was a present from a good friend of mine, an English artist, who understood and admired *Yamato Damashi*. It represents the last of our *ronin* (wave-men — loyal retainers who quitted their clan to avenge the wrongs of their lord). Our *daimio* was insulted by a brother-noble, and those gallant *samurai* avenged him."

"They look like cutthroats," murmured Fitz.

The gentleman smiled, bowed, and catching the sound of the words, replied,—

"Pardon me, they did not do that; they met him on his way from the Shogun's castle and took his head, which they presented to our chief on a *sambo* (stand of white wood). After performing the loyal deed, they committed *hari-kiri* (a form of suicide)."

Mrs. Jewett, who was horrified, glanced at her husband; but Sallie, who had listened with the greatest interest, said, —

"I understand, sir; they were great heroes, like the immortal Forty-seven."

"Daughter," murmured her mother, "what do you mean?"

Oto came to the rescue, remarking, —

"All that sort of thing is now abolished. Our nobles no longer have armed retainers to avenge their quarrels, but go to law like Americans. Those *ronin* only performed what they considered to be a sacred duty, and must not be confounded with ordinary assassins."

"Why did they wear baskets on their heads?" asked Fitz.

"To conceal their features," replied Oto. "I remember when the streets of Yedo (Tokio) swarmed with men wearing such hats."

"I have read of them," said Sallie. "I think they were just splendid."

"Daughter!" once more whispered her mother.

"Well, Roninism is a thing of the past," returned Oto. "My father values that picture because it represents *Yamato Damashi*, fidelity to the chief."

"Yes, yes," sighed their host. "Those were true *samurai*. They died like heroes."

"Who are these men in armor?" inquired Fitz, pointing to a large painting over the *tokonoma*.

"Ah!" exclaimed Mr. Nambo, bowing respectfully and sucking in his breath as he advanced. "This is a picture of

A DAIMIO AND HIS RETAINERS.

my old lord and his chief warriors. I am the person who is holding a bow."

"I don't think the artist flattered you any, sir," said Fitz. "He has given you a most unnatural smile."

RONINS IN AMBUSH.

"I wore a metal mask," was the quiet reply. "Ah! those were the times. Now our beloved chief has lost his title and wears foreign garments."

"They must feel more comfortable than those tin suits,"

said the irrepressible. "Why has he a paper duster in his hand?"

"That was his general's baton," proudly answered Mr. Nambo. "Helas! how he has been overcome by misfortunes!"

"Who is this gentleman?" demanded the boy, indicating a picture of a man in armor.

"That was a loyal and brave soldier of our clan, who fell in one of the first engagements of the late war," was the answer. "He could use his sword like a *samurai*, and run like a deer. I do not know what he would have done had he lived to see the changes that have occurred in the last few years."

"He might have run a *jin-riki-sha*," suggested Fitz.

"Hush!" breathed his mother.

A SOLDIER OF OLD JAPAN.

Mr. Nambo did not hear this remark, as he was busily engaged in looking at a curious painting on a *kakemono*. It represented a foreign-built ship, flying Japanese flags, and decorated with various insignia; while above, in the clouds, were extraordinary processions, such as are sometimes seen in our allegorical pictures.

"This," he said, "is a very great curiosity. It was painted by an artist in the service of the late Shogun. I picked it up very cheaply in a shop where they sell second-hand furniture."

AN ALLEGORICAL PICTURE.

"What is it all about?" asked Fitz.

"It represents the first trip made by the Shogun in a foreign-built steamer. You will observe that the after-part of the ship is enclosed with screens bearing the Tokugawa crest. In the clouds, on the right, sits the Shogun, on horseback, guarded by the principal gods, and before him goes a Tengu to drive away the evil spirits."

"What are those foxes doing on the left?" inquired Johnnie.

"Those are the guardians of Tokio, dressed as soldiers, and carrying *gohei*," said Mr. Nambo. "The artist put them in for the same reason that American painters depict your god of Victory in their historical works. This is a pictorial poem. The designer gave his imagination full play. I keep it more to remind me of the past than for its artistic merits."

Near the painting was a long scroll, on which was sketched a procession of men clothed in foreign uniforms.

"What is that?" asked Sallie.

Mr. Nambo smiled, and bowed repeatedly, then said,—

"That represents the landing of the first embassy from England. It was drawn by a young artist of Nagasaki, but is not quite correct in some of its details. He only had a passing

A JAPANESE CARICATURE.

glimpse of them as they marched by his house, and was obliged to copy the hats and banner from old pictures."

"It is very comical," remarked the Professor. "I wonder where he obtained that idea of the British flag?"

"From the Chinese," answered their host. "In those days our uneducated countrymen termed all foreigners Chinese."

Oto laughed, and said,—

"The Americans often confuse us with the people of that nation. There was a restaurant-keeper in Boston, who, whenever I visited his place, always asked me how my laundry was doing. One day, holding up a table-napkin, he inquired how much a dozen I charged to wash those articles."

"Didn't you get angry?" demanded Johnnie.

"No," was the good-humored reply. "He meant well. I

merely mentioned the circumstance to show that we are not the only people who misunderstand the nationality of our visitors."

"He must have been a Dutchman," muttered Fitz.

"He was," quietly returned Oto. "I never found a genuine American who mistook me for a Chinese."

"Why are those men carrying chairs behind the Envoy," inquired Sallie.

"That was very amusing," said Mr. Nambo. "The Envoy was determined he would not squat on the floor, in Japanese fashion, so had two gorgeous chairs carried by his servants. Of course our people made a great deal of fun about it."

"What did his officers do?" asked Johnnie.

"We provided them with camp-stools. There was no occasion for the Envoy to bring his own seats with him. He was a very pompous man, and made himself obnoxious to our officials. I am told that whenever they refused to agree to his propositions, he used to get red in the face, and say to the interpreter: 'Tell them if they don't come to my terms within twenty-four hours, I'll blow their country out of existence.'"

He related a number of amusing anecdotes about the first arrival of foreigners in Japan, and in many ways showed that, though he now professed to be a firm admirer of the new order of things, in his heart he revered the old.

That evening, as the visitors were proceeding to their rooms, Oto said to the Professor,—

"I fear you do not understand my father when he speaks so enthusiastically about the past, and refers in glowing terms to the actions of the *Ronin* of his clan. Our *daimio* was, and is, in every sense, a noble man. A few years ago nobody considered Roninism to be a crime. My father is gentle and humane, and would not give pain to any one."

"We perfectly comprehend his feelings, and admire his

loyalty to his chief," replied the Professor. "It is wonderful that he and men like him ever consented to put aside their swords."

"He did it at the command of our lord," said Oto. "I remember the day when our *daimio* assembled the *samurai* of the clan, and read the decree of the *Mikado* (emperor), commanding him to renounce his title and estates, and to retire into private life. He said: 'I ask you to transfer your allegiance to your rightful sovereign, and to serve him as faithfully as you have done me.' I am so glad you so thoroughly appreciate my parent."

After the boys had retired to their rooms, Fitz said to their companion, —

"How did that noble insult your lord?"

"In the performance of a solemn ceremony," said Oto. "I would prefer not to talk about the matter."

"Did he turn up his nose at him?" queried the irrepressible.

"No," said Oto. "Go to sleep."

Fitz remained quiet for about an hour, then began to turn in his bed, and groan as though suffering acute pain.

Oto, fearing his friend was sick, rose, and entering the chamber, said in a kindly tone, —

"What is the matter, old fellow?"

"I can't sleep," moaned Fitz. "I wish you would answer that question I asked you. I am just dying to know, and if you do not tell me I shan't close my eyes all night."

"I know the reason," said Johnnie, coming to Oto's rescue.

"Then why don't you tell me?" snapped Fitz, assuming an erect position. "I believe you like to torment a fellow, Johnnie Jewett."

His brother laughed sarcastically, and replied, —

"No doubt the lord's enemy asked an impudent question, and was punished for his pains."

"Yes," said Oto, "it was something of that kind. I am afraid if Fitz had lived in the olden times he would have been served like Awoyama-Tshihawa-Sakounisogen-Tdzoumi-no-Kami."

"Won't you translate that to me?" drowsily murmured Fitz, sinking backward. "Heigho!"

"Go to sleep, go to sleep," said Oto. "If you don't, I will fetch old Mitsu-ro, and make her give you a cup of medicine."

This threat took effect, and in a few moments the tongue of the merry boy had ceased to wag.

## CHAPTER XII.

### SCENES IN THE CAPITAL.

What are those strangly-clad beings
Who move quickly from one spot of interest to another
Like butterflies flitting from flower to flower?
These are Americans.
They are as restless as the ocean.
In one day they will learn more of a city
Than an inhabitant will in a year.
Are they not extraordinary persons?—JAPANESE POEM.

FOR the first few days after their arrival in Tokio, the travellers rested, and enjoyed the tranquil delights of a Japanese house.

One morning, Mrs. Jewett complained of the toothache, on hearing of which Mrs. Nambo entered her guest's room, and having condoled with her, gravely observed,—

"Why do you not stain your teeth? It is a sure cure for your trouble. Let me bring my dye-pot and brush, and apply the mixture. All our married ladies use it."

"No, thank you," replied Mrs. Jewett. "My husband would be shocked if I did such a thing. I notice, you also shave off your eyebrows."

"Yes," was the quiet response; "we used to shave our children's heads and eyebrows, but now the custom is going out of fashion. Ah! our young women are very foolish, they neglect their personal appearance and follow your custom. No wonder you have to employ an army of dentists."

She opened her mouth, and exhibited her teeth, which were as black as polished ebony.

As they were chatting they heard a cry outside, and presently Mitsu-ro entered, alternately beating her forehead, and clasping her hands palm to palm, as though in great agony of mind.

"What is the matter?" inquired her mistress.

"Oh!" moaned the old lady, "Fitz San has killed the servant of Inari Sama (the god-fox); the one that used to live under my room."

"What does she mean?" asked Mrs. Jewett.

"The god-fox! the god-fox!" sobbed Mitsu-ro. "His poor servant was only amusing himself with a chicken when your son murdered him with a stone. Some dreadful misfortune will surely overtake us! The poor servant!"

"May I come in, mother?" said the boy from the veranda.

"Yes, Fitz. What have you been doing?"

Fitz and Johnnie entered, and the former said, —

"We went out with Oto to feed the chicks, and he left us in order to procure some more rice. During his absence a fox leaped over the fence and seized a chicken, so I picked up a stone and knocked it over."

"It was the servant of our god-fox," sobbed Mitsu-ro.

"I am sorry," he frankly answered. "I did not know that you worshipped the creatures."

Mrs. Nambo comforted the old lady, and sent her out of the room; then whispered, as though afraid of being overheard, —

"She is very ignorant and superstitious. The fox is the local deity of Tokio, and is worshipped by the common people, who believe, if the animal puts a wisp of straw or a few ears of rice on its head, it can change itself into a human being. Of course we do not credit such nonsense. I wish our servants were like yours. Oto says your domestics have no such silly ideas."

"I am not so certain about that," replied Mrs. Jewett. "I have had help who were quite as superstitious as your old nurse. Fitz, you must not kill another fox."

"Certainly I will not, mother," he replied. "I am sorry I hurt the old lady's feelings."

When Oto heard of this he smiled, and said,—

"My foster-mother little knows that I have killed dozens of her pets. In my younger days I used to trap them in a double basket containing a live chicken. They are a perfect pest."

"Are they a worse nuisance than our neighbor's cats?" asked Johnnie.

"Well, I don't know," was the merry reply. "Though they steal everything they can carry off, they do not keep people awake all night."

"Why did your fellow-citizens choose a fox as their local deity?" demanded Fitz.

"We regard those creatures as your people do fairies," answered Oto. "Our ignorant classes believe in them, and deem them gods. It is said a fox led the original founder of Yedo to the site of the city. I'm glad Fitz killed the animal. The *betto* (groom) tells me it has stolen lots of my father's chickens. Come, boys, would you like to visit the great fish-market near the Nippon Bashi?"

They answered in the affirmative, and in a few moments entered their *jin-riki-sha*, and started for their destination.

As they rode down the avenue they met Izakura, Mr. Nambo's cook, who had just returned from marketing. His head was enveloped in a towel, and he carried in one hand a basket in which were some eggs, and in the other a bunch of bamboo fibre, used to clean dishes.

Bowing to his young master, he said,—

"The market is alive with customers. Go in by the north entrance, and take your friends to the main square, where the live fish are arriving from the bay. The honorable gentlemen will be much astonished. I have secured some beef and mutton for you, Mr. Oto."

He bowed and went off toward the kitchen, followed by a number of coolies carrying provisions.

"Izakura thinks it is dreadfully barbarous for me to eat meat," said their friend. "But he is a good fellow and an excellent cook."

Away they went down the avenue, the *jin-riki-sha* men racing one another, and seeming to enjoy the exercise.

As they were crossing a small bridge, they were compelled to halt until a drove of oxen had passed. While thus delayed, Johnnie asked Oto why the structure above them was furnished with water-gates.

"That is a remnant of the old times,"

IZAKURA.

he answered. "Those gates were closed every night to prevent thieves from passing the canals. Now the police patrol the water-courses, and the gates are gradually going to decay."

After a pleasant ride they arrived at the entrance to the fish-market, and, dismissing their *jin-riki-sha*, threaded their way among the noisy crowd.

The open space was occupied by peddlers who shouted the names of their wares, and urged the visitors to buy; and the sheds surrounding it were filled with wholesale dealers and auctioneers.

Men carrying enormous fish on their bare shoulders, coolies staggering along under the weight of big sharks suspended from bamboo bearing-sticks, and nude runners laden with live carp that did not make any show of resistance, jostled each other, and yelled vociferously. Oto told his companions that the fishermen and persons who unloaded the boats were permitted to work *en déshabille*.

The place was thronged with purchasers, a few of whom were women of the lower class.

The boys approached a platform on which were heaped dolphin, shark, halibut, flounders, cod, conger-eels, and other large fish, flanked with tubs containing oysters, mussels, clams, sea-eggs, and a number of turtle, which the proprietor was auctioning in a very novel manner.

Taking an enormous skate by a string passed through its gills, he raised it a little, and shouted, —

"Hundred *sen !* hundred ! ninety-nine ! ninety-eight ! ninety-seven ! "

When he reached a figure that suited his customers, the latter held up their hands, doubling all but two fingers. Those who were anxious to buy, but who were awaiting a lower price, held up their hands, fingers down.

From his stall they went to a side street, where the women were making purchases. Fitz counted over seventy varieties of fish on exhibition, among them being whale and shark. This number did not include the shell species, of which they noticed over twenty sorts.

Every part of some kinds, such as cod, is eaten, even the gills and intestines; the latter being made into a very delicate tripe, much esteemed by epicures.

The proprietors of the stalls sat on raised platforms in the rear of their wares, watching their employés and entering sales in their books.

On one stall the boys saw many bushels of *echini* (sea-urchins, or sea-eggs). These appeared to be in great demand. Oto informed them that only a portion of this fish was used for food, the rest being considered poisonous.

Among the curiosities of the market were party-colored fish, brilliant in red, blue, and gold tints, sold alive in glass and porcelain jars. These beautiful creatures capture flies by spouting water over them. The boys also saw any quantity of tiger-marked sea-porcupines and zebra-soles, both of which are eaten by the natives.

While they were watching the scene, the marketmen continued to arrive with enormous fishes, which were dumped upon mats, placed on the ground, and cut up with long, strong knives.

After minutely inspecting the fresh-fish department, the lads visited the side streets, devoted to the sale of the dried sorts, — among these being oysters, shrunk out of all shape, mussels, sardines, clams, shrimps, cod, whale, and shark.

On the outskirts of the market were many shops and open stalls, devoted to the preparation and sale of cuttle-fish.

The boys halted before a stand where a man was frying the delicacy and chatting to a coolie, who was waiting for a load. The vender seeing Oto, said, —

" Honorable sir, do you wish to buy some tender slices? I have purchased a cuttle weighing a hundred pounds, and can furnish you with any part of the fish, either fresh or cooked."

" Do you eat those things? " asked Fitz.

" Eat them! " cried the man, " why, they are much sought after and are most delicate in flavor."

"I thought they lived on human beings," said Johnnie.

" Yeh! " shouted the fellow. " So do sharks, shrimps, cod, and all fishes, when they get a chance. You foreigners eat cows and drink milk, yet turn up your noses at such luxuries as a tender cuttle-fish. Yeh! "

" Come away," said Oto; " he is a rude man."

They quitted the market, and visited the quarter devoted to the slaughter of cattle. As they approached the spot, they saw

THE GREAT FISH-MARKET OF TOKIO.

carts laden with baskets of charcoal and drawn by oxen, which Oto said were, like the fuel, brought in for sale.

A pilgrim passed them, ringing his bell, and they noticed some lightly-dressed coolies carrying boxes containing knives.

"Those are the butchers," said their friend. "They are permitted to go about the markets in that manner."

THE VENDERS OF CUTTLE-FISH.

Women were driving in beeves, and the stalls were rapidly being filled with water-buffaloes and foreign cattle.

The boys crossed a plank bridge, and entered a large enclosure filled with covered pens, containing many hundred head of cattle.

Here they were met by an official, who, seeing the young Americans, said, —

"What do you think of our show? We slaughtered a thousand oxen and three hundred sheep last week, and have orders for more meat than we can supply. We are now beginning to kill pigs, and if all our people take to eating animal food, shall have to enlarge our premises."

"Where does your supply come from?" asked Fitz.

"From the government stock-farm, from Shanghai and

THE CATTLE-MARKET.

Yezo," answered the man. "Those water-buffaloes are from the adjoining country. When the farmers have worked them almost to death, they bring them here with a load of wood, which we buy with the cattle."

"Isn't their flesh almost as tough as their hides?" demanded Fitz.

"Well, yes," replied their informant. "It is not very

tender. The government buys it for the army, navy, and public institutions."

"Yes," laughingly observed Oto. "That is the sort of tenderloin they gave us at the Imperial College."

"Where are your meat stores?"

"We only kill the animals for the retail dealers. The slaughtering is done at night, and the carcasses and refuse are removed by daylight."

After the boys had satisfied their curiosity, they sauntered into a neighboring street, from which proceeded sounds of a drum and the noise of a crowd.

"That must be the Lion of the Corea," said Oto. "When I was a little fellow I used to like to watch his antics."

As they turned the corner they beheld a gigantic figure, the head and body of which towered above the spectators. Before him ran a number of boys, and behind were three musicians and a dozen nurse-girls, with children on their backs, who, like the boys, shouted, —

"Hai, old lion!"

"Come," said Oto, halting near one of the gateways of a ward division, in front of which was a large lantern, decorated with a *tomoye* (lucky character); "there is a school down that street, and the acrobats are sure to perform here."

On came the lion, who, emerging from the crowd, advanced toward them, and revealed beneath his striped cloak a pair of grimy hands employed in beating a tambour, the lower portion of a human body clothed in a blue cotton robe, and a pair of sturdy, muscular limbs, the feet of which were protected with straw sandals.

The musician with the drum beat his instrument, the flute-player blew until his cheeks were distended like those of a person suffering from the mumps, and the third player banged his tambour, and glanced at the young Americans, as though anticipating a good fee.

The lion danced very much in the style of a trained bear, raised and lowered his head-piece,—which was fixed upon a bamboo inserted in a socket secured to his back,—shouted, roared, and growled, in a manner ridiculous enough to amuse any one; his gestures and capers eliciting yells of approval

THE LION OF COREA DANCING.

from the audience, who, child-like, called him various names and treated him with half-timid familiarity.

As he was jumping around and diverting them with his contortions, a number of lads came rushing from the side street, and, upon nearing him, began to shout,—

"Hai, old lion. I hope your excellency is well! Dance lively, now we've come! We're the boys who have the coin. Kick higher; you are not half as smart as the other lion who came here a moon ago."

The performer, thus adjured. redoubled his endeavors, while

his orchestra banged, blew, and thumped their instruments; as they did so, uttering shrill cries of encouragement.

The new-comers were as full of monkey-tricks as the acrobat. They threw somersaults in front of him, yelled, pulled at his robe, and, darting at him, inflicted pinches on his limbs that presently roused his temper, and caused him to retaliate with sundry kicks, which in some instances were received by his followers.

"Hai — hai — hai!" they shouted. "*Ha-yaku!*" (hurry up.)

The lion replied by lowering his head, pulling a string, and advancing with open mouth, at the same time uttering most hideous noises. However, the children did not appear to mind his demonstration, and continued to yell, scream, and amuse themselves as before.

In the midst of this fun, a bald-headed teacher, carrying in his left hand a paper duster, suddenly emerged from a building on the side street, and called angrily to the boys, saying, —

"What means this? Are you not aware it is the hour of study?"

At the sound of their instructor's voice the urchins stopped their fun, and assuming a respectful demeanor, prepared to retire, though the Americans noticed that none of them went off without giving the lion a few *sen*.

"There is nothing small or mean about the average Japanese boy," said Fitz. "When he has been amused by a performer, he pays his money like a little man."

As the scholars were making off, their master said to the lion, who was resting from his labor, —

"You ought to have more sense than to keep children from their studies. If this sort of thing is repeated, I shall report the matter to the authorities."

"Most excellent teacher," politely replied the man, "you

do us great injustice. We had no idea we were detaining your scholars."

"Very well; do not repeat the offence," grumbled the preceptor. "I will overlook your fault this time."

"I hope your excellency will have good health," said the performer. "Your pupils are perfect young gentlemen."

After the old fellow was out of hearing, the orchestra recommenced its din, and the lion indulged in a pantomimic dance expressive of defiance, which appeared to afford the bystanders the greatest amusement, and elicited shouts of laughter from some people who were watching him from the porch of a neighboring building. On seeing them, he once more arranged the bamboo in the socket secured to his back, took the string of his tambour between his teeth, and pulling down his lion's robe, grasped his sticks, and began to posture and drum as before, while his assistants moved among the crowd, and collected money on their fans.

Although, at first glance, he appeared to caper at his own sweet will, the boys soon discovered that he performed certain steps, which were methodically grotesque, clumsy, coarse, and, no doubt, of ancient origin.

The lion danced until his patrons refused to contribute another coin, upon discovering which he partly removed his make-up, and, with his companions, squatted near the big lantern, where the young Americans had a good opportunity to examine his features. He was probably between thirty and forty years old, and was muscular and sturdy. His lion-skin was made of paper and hemp, his mask of papier-mâché painted and gilded, and his mane of long strips of tough paper, colored yellow and brown. He sat on the ground, sucking at his tiny-bowled brass pipe, and perspiring freely; before him were his tambour and bamboo-sticks. As the boys approached he glanced up, and, blinking his bilious-looking eyes, said, —

"I hope your excellencies have approved of my humble performance?"

They replied that they had been much entertained; and after questioning him awhile, he said,—

THE LION REFRESHING HIMSELF.

"How came I in this business? Ah, that is a long story. My parents died when I was about as big as my drum, and left me to the tender mercy of a relative, by whom I was sold to an acrobat. The latter kicked me into shape, and took me everywhere, training myself and two other miserable orphans as he would have done three apes. When he died I started business as a Lion of the Corea, and "— laughing —" here I am!"

"How much do you make a day?" asked Fitz.

"Ah! now you puzzle me," he merrily replied. "Sometimes we collect quite a sum, at others only earn our fish and rice, and, if luck is against us, not even our salt. We are always fortunate when we meet your foreign excellencies, who pay us like noblemen."

After this strong hint, there was nothing for the strangers but to open their purses and give him a gratuity. This brought the entire party to their feet, and set them capering and drumming; whereupon Oto and his friends made off, leaving the crowd to enjoy the result of their liberality.

"Come," said Oto, "I know a first-class French restaurant near here,—suppose we have breakfast. Our folks have taken theirs long ago."

They followed him, and found themselves in an elegantly furnished saloon, the walls of which were adorned with foreign paintings and engravings.

"There are many such places in Tokio," remarked Oto. "Please order what you like."

When the repast was finished, and the bill brought, he paid the amount, seven dollars; noticing which, Johnnie said,—

"We could have breakfasted in a Japanese restaurant for fifty *sen* each, and had a better meal. After this we will not patronize foreign establishments."

Oto laughed, and said,—

"You are right. I know it is foolish to pay a foreigner seven dollars for what one of our people can supply for a dollar and a half."

Johnnie and Fitz insisted on sharing the expense, after which they quitted the place, and renewed their rambles, presently finding themselves once more in the vicinity of the Nippon Bashi. Hearing the murmur of a crowd and the "ping, ping" of a *samisen* (guitar), they followed the sound, and soon arrived at an open space where four streets met, in which they beheld a number of acrobats and jugglers performing to an admiring audience.

On their left was a clog-maker staining the wooden articles with a broad, flat brush, which he dipped in a black liquid; as he did so, mingling his shouts of approval with those of the other spectators.

The space chosen was near a ward-gate, right in the centre of the traffic; and on the left were a range of open-fronted stores, occupied by toy-makers, clock-manufacturers, tailors, and pipe-makers, who worked quite calmly, and did not appear to notice the exhibitors: a sword-juggler, two acrobats, and a shrill-voiced dame, who played the *samisen*, and encouraged the artists with her words and gestures.

Notwithstanding the presence of ladies, the acrobats had reduced their costume to one of primitive simplicity—in fact, to mere harness.

After a few preliminaries, one of the men thrust a naked sword down his throat, and invited the spectators to feel the point under the skin below his ribs. This appeared to greatly interest the servant-girls and children, who were loud in their exclamations of wonder and approval. He advanced with

STREET ACROBATS.

extended hands, and requested Fitz to satisfy himself that he had swallowed the weapon; then he drew the blade from his throat and refreshed himself with a cup of tea. In reply to the boy's questions, he stated his age was thirty, and that he belonged to the province of Yamato. He declined to repeat the performance, or to permit them to closely examine the sword, saying he had a sore throat, and it was not respectful to exhibit a naked weapon.

While the young Americans were chatting with him, his companions had set up a stick, on which they vertically balanced two hoops and a porcelain bottle. They also produced a long, bottomless basket, made of split bamboo, such as is used for carrying wild animals to market. This they set on two low horses of wood, like a saw-buck.

The sword-swallower excused himself, and, directing their attention to his associates, retired, when they saw one of the acrobats, whose head was bound with a towel, and who carried a pipe and tobacco-pouch thrust in his girdle, step back in the direction of the gate. Lowering his head, he ran toward the hoops, and springing from the ground, darted through them without disturbing the bottle, hoops, or stick on which the latter stood.

After this the third man, who was even more simply clothed than his comrades, backed among the crowd, and, at a signal from his wife, ran forward and darted through the basket without touching it in any way. He landed upon his hands, threw a somersault, and, dropping upon his knees, bowed respectfully to the young Americans, crying,—

"A little encouragement, your excellencies! Mine is very hard work!"

The boys rewarded him; then his wife placed three lighted candles in the basket, and he repeated his jump in the same dexterous manner.

The crowd soon became so dense that the strangers were compelled to quit the spot, and, entering *jin-riki-sha*, were conveyed home, where they found their parents discussing a visit to the famous temple of Asakusa.

"The chrysanthemums are in full bloom," said Mrs. Nambo. "I think if the boys are not too tired we will start after the mid-day meal. Asakusa is only a short distance, and we can walk there."

About two o'clock the Professor and his family, Mr. and Mrs. Nambo, Oto and O-Kiku started for the world-renowned temple.

"Now, Fitz," whispered Mrs. Jewett, "try and keep your thoughts to yourself. Though our friends take your remarks very kindly, I am sure they must sometimes feel hurt by them."

"I'll try," he answered.

## CHAPTER XIII.

#### THE TEMPLE OF KUWANNON AT ASAKUSA.

> From January to December
> Asakusa contains ten thousand delights.
> As the months return we behold
> The camellia, plum-blossom, cherry-bloom,
> Peony, lotus, azalea, and chrysanthemum,
> And always the lovely evergreens.
> Let us go to Asakusa
> To pray to Kuwannon, and to see the flowers.
> JAPANESE POEM.

MRS. NAMBO quoted the foregoing to Mrs. Jewett as they walked toward their destination, adding gently,—

"I suppose you will not pray to Kuwannon?"

Before the lady could reply, Fitz came to her rescue, saying,—

"Mother won't, but I don't mind firing a few shots."

"Fitz, Fitz," she whispered, "remember what you promised;" then, turning to her hostess, said, "You all appear to be fond of poetry. Who was Kuwannon? Will you tell me something about him?"

"Kuwannon is a goddess," replied Mrs. Nambo, who was always ready to impart information about her faith. "She was born in China nearly three thousand years ago. Her father desired her to marry, and on her refusing ordered her to be decapitated. The sword of the executioner shivered across her neck, and did not harm her, so she was condemned to be smothered. When her spirit reached the abode of the unhappy, its presence rendered the place so enjoyable and beautiful that Ema placed her on a lotus-flower, and sent her back to earth and life. Soon after Kuwannon's return her father fell sick, whereupon she fed him with the flesh of her arms. The authorities gave orders for a statue to be erected to her, but the sculptor, instead of merely representing her with two arms, gave her a thousand."

"She must look like a forty-bladed penknife," muttered Fitz.

His mother frowned, and Mrs. Nambo continued, —

"For many centuries there was no temple to her in Tokio; however, one day a Ronin noble, who, in order to earn his rice, was reduced to fish in the Sumida River, was hauling in his net, when he found in it only a small figure of Kuwannon, which he returned to the stream. He repeated his cast in a number of places, and always drew in the same figure. Struck by this singular occurrence, he quitted fishing, and taking the goddess to a shrine that stood near the present temple, deposited it, and from that grew the mighty fabric we now call the Temple of Kuwannon."

"What became of the lone fisherman?" inquired Johnnie.

"He renounced his occupation, turned *bozu*, and died a saint," replied their informant.

"I reckon it paid him better than fishing," observed Fitz to his sister, in a low tone.

Sallie was about to reply, when they entered the main street, and beheld the principal gateway of the temple grounds.

The crowd was a sight in itself, and was so dense that the party had great difficulty in keeping together. Imperial soldiers and sailors in foreign uniforms, gentlemen and ladies in full national dress, children, nurses, beggars, showmen, peddlers, and foreigners, were moving to and fro; the greater number, like the Jewetts, being bound for the temple.

On the right was the Sumada River, spanned by a stone structure, termed the Adzuma Bridge, which was black with human beings.

The travellers halted at a wayside restaurant, opposite the main entrance, and, as they sipped their tea, watched the animated scene.

The air was full of strange odors and noises, above which rose the cries of peddlers who squatted in groups under the trees, or mingled with the spectators.

On the right, a blind beggar with a monkey clinging to his back, was making his way toward the main avenue, followed by a number of boys, who shouted, —

"*S-aru-hito! s-aru-hito!*" (Monkey-man! monkey-man!)

One youth, bolder than the rest, attempted to capture the animal by placing a hoop, secured to a stick, over its head, whereupon the monkey sprang at his tormentor and bit him several times, then dropped to the ground, and, scampering after his master, soon regained his old position.

Venders were selling miniature fireworks, which they ignited on the palms of their hands, or while secured by a string to their arms, these dangerous toys appearing greatly to delight the children.

Nearly all the salesmen on the sidewalks exhibited advertisements, and were provided with short bamboos, which they used to punish pilferers.

Some of the dealers sold straw toys, made in the shape of tortoises and animals; others, pipes for blowing soap-bubbles; and a number vended cakes and told fortunes; the seers being provided with a marionnette, which they moved by strings attached to their toes.

The roadway was watered by men carrying large buckets suspended from long poles; the bottoms of the vessels being finely perforated, so as to permit the liquid to escape freely. These useful laborers wore very scanty raiment, and were not supposed to go outside the temple grounds.

"Come," said Mr. Nambo, as his friends rose to quit the

restaurant. "We will first view the shows, then visit the temple, and afterwards inspect the flowers."

"We are at your disposal," replied the Professor. "You lead, and we will follow."

By that time the mass of people had passed through the gateway, and the travellers were enabled to keep tolerably close together.

"Say," cried Johnnie, pointing to a conjurer performing before a little booth on which were displayed some apparatus, "let us see what he is going to do."

THE SWORD TRICK. (*From a Japanese Picture.*)

The man placed three *sambo*, one on top of the other, thrust his toes into a pair of high clogs, and taking a long sword, stepped on to the summit of the pile, and proceeded to spin a top on the edge of the weapon. He next ran a fan up and down the blade, threw it into the air, and caught it on the point, finally, tossing it with a peculiar jerk, slashed at it as it descended, and divided the article into two fragments, which changed into birds and were blown away.

Fitz secured one of the pieces, and found it was ingeniously constructed of bamboo and paper.

THE AVENUE OF ASAKUSA.

After giving the man a gratuity, they passed on, and watched the performance of some athletes in a splendidly decorated booth, the front of which was enclosed with wooden posts about three feet high.

There was quite a company of artists in this exhibition, and it was evidently one of the features of the place.

Patrons, who paid an extra fee, were permitted to enter a space railed off from the crowd.

The troupe consisted of three men and two boys, all of whom appeared to be boneless. Their performances were enlivened by a band of three musicians, who also sang, and from time to time yelled encouragement to their employers. On seeing the foreigners, the chief acrobat, who was dressed in flowing robes, sprang upon the posts in front of the place, and performed some astounding feats,— at one time supporting his entire company on his shoulders. He seemed to be quite at his ease, and, as he balanced, fanned himself, and directed his assistants.

Presently one of the men, who was clad in body-armor, produced a pole, to the top of which was fastened a banner. At a signal from their leader, one of the boys climbed the staff, and, resting his toes on the cross-piece, extended himself at an angle from it, crying,—

"Hai! hai! hai!"

While he was hanging in this position, the other lad mounted a pyramid of *sambo* and boxes, and grasped the top one with his hands, then elevated his feet, and slowly lowered them until the soles rested on his shaven pate.

"Jeminy!" cried Fitz, "he's standing on his own head!"

At that instant the third man, who was carefully holding a curious, sword-like article, uttered a loud, prolonged yell, when the apparatus burst into a dozen pieces, — each fragment being a top in full spin.

ACROBATS.

The musicians screamed frantically, and played as though their lives depended upon their vigor; then the manager, dropping from his perch, bowed to the Americans and said, —

"Honorable strangers from afar, I trust you are pleased with our humble endeavors."

"I have a headache," said Mrs. Jewett, as the gentlemen rewarded the performers. "Suppose we continue our walk."

They quitted the booth, and, entering the grounds, advanced up a long paved avenue to the grand entrance of the temple, a colossal, double-roofed *mon* (gateway), painted red, near which were stalls for the sale of rosaries and metal idols to be worn in the bosom or sleeves. These were piled in heaps along with memorial tablets, portable shrines, sacred bells, and candlesticks.

"What are those things?" asked Johnnie, indicating the enormous figures on his right and left, under the gateway.

"They are the Ni-o (two kings)," replied Mr. Nambo. "The red statue, with its mouth open, represents the *Yo*, male, or warm principle of nature. The green one, with its mouth firmly closed, is the *In*, female, or cold."

Oto, who did not believe in the *Yo* and *In*, was anxious to hurry onward, but Fitz would not stir. He pretended to be deeply interested in the hideous images, and was about to ask why the female figure had its mouth so firmly closed, when his father said, —

"Come, my son, you have looked at those long enough. We will enter the temple."

As the lads followed the adults into the main courtyard, Fitz pinched Oto, and whispered, —

"You know I am just dying to learn why that female figure has her mouth shut — it isn't natural. There must be some mystery about it, and I think it is mean of you not to tell me."

"It signifies that our women know how to keep silent," was the response. "The *In* means stillness, and *Yo* noise."

"*Yo* also means the first person singular, does it not?" inquired Oto's tormentor.

"Yes, yes; and it means a young boy," said Johnnie. "If the Japanese want a god of inquisitiveness, they ought to make a statue of you."

"My!" chuckled the irrepressible. "That's a tri-angular pun! *Yo* (I), *Yo* (noise), *Yo* (a youth)."

While they were speaking, a crowd came rushing out of the temple, and began to swarm round the great pillars of the porch, noticing which, the Professor and Mr. Nambo halted, and the latter bade the party watch an old *bozu* and his two assistants, who had mounted a hanging-shelf, secured to the massive shaft by copper rods.

The *bozu* had his sleeves and the bosom of his robes filled with strips of paper, and his companions were provided with enormous fans.

When the ladder by which they had ascended was removed, and the gigantic lanterns on the left of the platform had ceased to sway, the *bozu* advanced to the edge of the platform, and intoned, —

"*Namu, Amida, Butsu!*"

Hearing these words, the mass of humanity beneath him knelt and bowed their heads to the ground, or rather attempted to do so. Then rose a sound like the murmur of an approaching storm, which quickly culminated in a cry of, —

"*Nammiyo! Nammiyo! Nammiyo!*"

In another moment the people were again on their feet, yelling and extending their hands frantically towards the platform.

The old *bozu*, whose calm, almost cynical face contrasted strongly with the excited features of his congregation, glanced down upon them, and, thrusting his hands into the bosom of his robe, drew forth a package of papers, which he tossed into the air.

These documents were quickly dispersed by his attendants, who, by a dexterous wave of their fans, sent the strips in all directions.

An exciting scene followed; men, women, and children struggling and screaming in their anxiety to get possession of the coveted documents, which were supposed to confer good fortune upon the possessors.

The Americans, seeing it would be some time before they could enter the temple, consulted with Mr. Nambo as to what was best to be done, and, while they were discussing the matter, Fitz pointed to the gratings in front of the figures in the gateway, and said to Oto, —

"Why do people tie their old sandals to that place, and — say, who wore those big ones?"

"Those are offerings from convalescent persons," snapped Oto. "You know that as well as I do."

"Well, but—" persisted the tease, "what sort of disease did they have to make them require such enormous sandals? They are a yard long and two feet wide. And why do yonder old women beat those wooden clappers?" — indicating some crones who were sitting near the gate, offering to pray for any one who would pay them a few *sen*. "And, Oto, why do those people wash their hands and rinse their mouths at that cistern?"

His friend did not reply.

"Let us buy a few peas for the pigeons," said Miss Kiku, who was secretly amused at her cousin's annoyance. "The sacred birds are frightened at the noise, and have retired to their nests in the roof of the porch."

The boys walked over to some stands kept by ancient-looking dames, who sold grain for the birds.

DISTRIBUTING CHARMS. PORCH OF THE TEMPLE.

...ght a saucer of peas, and Sallie and the boys ... heavily; but though they scattered their offerings ...usion, not a pigeon stirred.

...while the distribution of charms was continued, and ...e had become almost deafening.

"We had better go and see the sacred ponies," suggested .s. Nambo.

They followed her to a stable on the left of the temple, and saw two pink-eyed, white animals, so bloated from over-feeding that they looked like incipient hippopotami.

The girl in charge of the steeds urged the visitors to purchase corn with which to feed the steeds, on hearing which Fitz cried, —

"Look out!"

The attendant gazed at him with alarm, and nervously demanded, —

"What is the matter?"

"Don't you give those ponies another *grain*," he said.

"Why not?" she anxiously inquired. "Honorable sir, tell me what you mean?"

He looked so serious that the spectators who had arrived before his party, and had bought some rice for the creatures, stared at him in amazement, and his father demanded in English, —

"What is the matter now, Fitz?"

"I was only warning the young lady not to allow the poor things to take any more food," was the reply. "Just look at them, sir; they are so full now they can scarcely breathe. If the pilgrims give them another grain they'll burst."

"Fitz, Fitz," said his mother, "those are sacred animals; you must not ridicule them."

When this was translated to Mr. Nambo, he laughed, and told the attendant, who giggled, and said, —

"Oh, that is too comical!"

"Remember what you promised me, Fitz," whispered his mother. "You ought to try and make yourself agreeable to our friends."

"Yes, ma'am," he replied. "I wasn't making fun that time, I can assure you. Just look at the unfortunate creatures. Mr. Bergh ought to see them."

When the *bozu* had exhausted all his charms, the crowd re-entered the temple, and he was assisted down from his lofty position.

"Now," said Mr. Nambo, "we shall have an opportunity to see the image of Kuwannon. Please follow me. I did not remember this was a festival, or we would have delayed our visit until to-morrow."

The party worked their way up the copper-edged steps, and by dint of pushing and elbowing, contrived to enter the main edifice, which was densely packed with worshippers.

Just inside the door was an enormous, bronze censer, surmounted by a sky-dog, and decorated with the twelve signs (hours). A pungent, bluish vapor ascended through the perforations in the cover, and the supply of incense was continually being replaced by the devotees, who purchased parcels of the perfumed grains from a toothless dame stationed near by.

Mrs. Nambo bought a small package, and emptied its contents into the burner, but neither her niece nor husband followed her example; however, Fitz, who was much attracted by the performance, and whose face denoted the satisfaction derived from a newly conceived idea, bought a large box, containing about two pounds of the powder, and, before his friends knew of his investment, scattered his offering on the live coals. The result was a choking, dense smoke that poured out of the holes in the censer, and almost suffocated the people near it.

Some Japanese soldiers in natty French uniforms, who were waiting to make their offerings, coughed, choked, and uttered muffled imprecations, and the crowd sneezed, hawked, and finally dispersed; everybody being anxious to get into the fresh air. In the midst of the confusion, a *bozu* came forward and after vigorously cuffing the incense-seller, cried, —

"Do you want to smother us all?"

The agitated dame pointed to Fitz.

"What have you done, sir?" sternly demanded the Professor, who suspected his son was at the bottom of the mischief.

"I?" innocently answered the boy. "I only burnt a little incense. Mother said I was to make myself agreeable. I have not done any harm."

His parent explained the matter to the *bozu*, who smiled, bowed, and said, —

"A thousand pardons. We thought the worthy woman was out of her mind. She sometimes gives such large pinches that the odor becomes quite overpowering. Would your honorable son like to burn a little more?"

The boy was about to acquiesce, when his father, after bowing to the *bozu*, addressed him sternly, saying, —

"Fitz, I am very much annoyed with you! Come, we will go and see the chrysanthemums."

As they emerged into the well-kept garden on the left of the temple, Miss Kiku said in a pleading tone, —

"Please don't scold Fitz. He did not mean to do wrong."

"He is very thoughtless," said the Professor. Then, turning to his hostess, he continued, "Mrs. Nambo, I am exceedingly sorry—"

"Indeed, you need not apologize," said the delighted old lady, whose eyes were still red from the effects of the incense. "I think he performed a very pious—"

"What lovely chrysanthemums!" exclaimed Oto, as though he had not heard his mother's remark. "Are they not a glorious sight?"

Miss Kiku bit her lips, and glanced at her cousin, and the visitors, who were glad to change the subject, joined Oto in his praise of the flowers.

"Beautiful! beautiful!" exclaimed Sallie. "Oh! such colors and magnificent blossoms! Why, they excel anything we have at home."

"Surely not," quietly replied Oto.

"Yes, they do!" said Johnnie. "You beat us at this sort of thing. Why, some of them are trained to grow in shapes; there's a cuttle-fish — and a lantern — and — a — fox!"

"Yes, they are lovely," said Mrs. Nambo. "We value the *kiku* (chrysanthemum) very highly. Its flower forms the imperial *mon*, and it has always been a favorite object for our artists to paint. Our poets have written thousands of stanzas about it. Fitz Sama, do you not think they are beautiful?"

"Are these the kind that you make greens of?" he asked.

"What!" said Sallie, who was perfectly horrified at the idea of converting such lovely objects into food.

"You need not say 'what' in that tone," he retorted. "Miss Kiku asked me whether I had ever tasted a dish of chrysanthemum flowers. I suppose a thing may be good to eat as well as nice to look at."

The young Japanese lady smiled, and said, —

"Fitz is quite right. We sometimes eat the yellow chrysanthemum blossoms, and I can assure you they make an excellent dish."

The visitors inspected the glorious masses, some of which contained over a thousand blooms, then they wandered about the grounds, and viewed the various articles of interest. The place was too full of visitors to render locomotion comfortable, and the Professor and his party were glad enough to find a quiet nook where they could enjoy tea and refreshments.

"Can't we see the wax-works?" inquired Johnnie.

"Do you mean the thirty-five tableaux of the miracles of Kuwannon?" said Mr. Nambo.

"Yes, sir; Oto always called them the wax-works."

Mr. Nambo regarded his son with a comical expression, as he answered,—

"The building will be packed with sightseers, so I think we must defer our visit until another day. I was not aware that my son described those sacred groups as wax-works."

They remained in the grounds until the evening, when the temples were brilliantly illuminated, and the whole place appeared alive with pleasure-seekers.

As they passed through the avenue on their way home, they beheld acrobats performing in the open air, and heard the shrill cries of *"Nammiyo! Nammiyo!"* mingled with the "hai! hai!" of athletes who were carrying pyramids of their brethren.

"We shall have to visit Asakusa again," remarked the Professor. "What say you, wife, shall we come early to-morrow and stay all day? I could wander for a week among those beautiful flowers."

NIGHT SCENE OUTSIDE THE TEMPLE.

## CHAPTER XIV.

#### FROM TOKIO TO KANASAWA.

When the days are warm
And the streets of Tokio glow like furnaces,
We will seek the cool groves
Of distant Kamakoura,
And the mountains of Hakone. — JAPANESE POEM.

THE next morning when the brothers awoke, Oto entered their room, and, drawing aside the *amado* (shutters), pointed to the sky, which was "emptying its liquid blessing" upon the scene.

"No travelling to-day," he said.

"Oto," replied Fitz, sitting up and rubbing his eyes, "I have been thinking of something."

"I hope it is something sensible," said his brother in a drowsy tone.

"Of course it is," was the merry rejoinder. "I'm not like you, Johnnie Jewett. I'm wide awake. Say, Oto, suppose, after this, we dress in Japanese fashion. When you came to the States you adopted our costume, and I notice that very few of your countrymen have discarded the national garb."

"To tell the truth, I would like to resume my old costume," answered Oto. "If Johnnie will agree to it we'll send for a tailor and have suits made right away."

"I'm willing," said Johnnie. "You wore our dress, so I do not see why we should not pay you a similar compliment."

That morning they held a secret consultation with some tradesmen, who were closeted with them for several hours, and who the next evening returned to the house with a number of

JAPANESE CEMETERY.

boxes containing everything necessary for the costumes of the three boys.

Sallie, who had been very anxious to know what her brothers were planning, endeavored to learn from Fitz, but the only reply he gave was, —

"You just wait, sister. We are going to astonish you."

The rain continued for three days, and seemed as though it would never cease. However, on the fourth morning the boys saw the sun shining through the crevices in the shutters, noticing which they hurriedly rose and dressed themselves in their new garments.

The suits consisted of silken under-shirts, cut low in the neck (Johnnie's idea), *kimono* (long coats), *hakama* (full trousers), and *obi* (girdles), of striped silk, white cotton *tabi* (socks with toe-pieces), and neatly made wooden clogs; the latter of course not being worn in the house.

When old Mitsu-ro beheld them, she clapped her hands, and exclaimed, —

"Oh! honorable foreign master-boys, do have your heads shaven on top and your hair dressed in proper fashion."

"Not for Fitz!" answered the irrepressible.

"Or for Johnnie," said his brother.

They waited till breakfast was announced, then entered the room in single file, and, prostrating themselves, performed the respectful ceremony, that is, bowed their foreheads nine times to the matted floor, and audibly inhaled their breath.

Every one was much amused, and Mrs. Nambo said, —

"You look very handsome in your new clothes. Please never resume those unbecoming —"

"I thought my honorable mother would be pleased," said Oto, speaking in time to prevent his mother from fully expressing her opinion about the foreign-cut garments. "Where is Sallie?"

As he spoke, the young lady, dressed in Japanese costume, advanced from her room, followed by O-Kiku.

"Why, sissy!" cried Fitz, "you look perfectly elegant."

"You did not imagine I meant to be outdone by you, did you, Fitz Jewett?" she laughingly replied. "O-Kiku and I guessed what you boys were about, and I made my mind up to do the same."

After breakfast a number of double *jin-riki-sha* were brought round to the entrance, and their host said, —

"I have engaged these vehicles in order that our friends might ride in company. The runners are very powerful men, and can pull twice the weight of ordinary ones. When you have selected your companions, we will start for Kanasawa, where we will rest for the night."

The Professor chose his wife; Mrs. Nambo, O-Kiku; Mr. Nambo, Oto; and Johnnie, Fitz, — Sallie electing to ride Abraham Lincoln, who was growing lazy from want of exercise.

They stepped into the *jin-riki-sha*, the shafts of which were resting on the ground, and the runners, raising the poles, gave the vehicles a tilt backwards and started at a run.

Away went the merry party, out of the main gate, along the avenue, over the Nippon Bashi, and past the castle walls; the moats surrounding which were glowing with lotus blossoms.

A short distance beyond, they halted to permit a procession to pass.

The buildings in that quarter were of two stories, and were draped with cloths imprinted with crests, and filled with spectators anxiously awaiting the arrival of the cortège.

"Come," said Mr. Nambo, who had alighted, "I have secured tickets of admission behind the railings on the side of the street. We shall have a good view of the sight, though only a part of the procession will pass here."

When they were comfortably seated on the matted ground,

THE FESTIVAL OF YORIMITSU.

they heard a great noise in the distance, and finally beheld a body of men advancing with a frame-work, sustaining a banner marked, " The Brotherhood of the Invincible Yorimitsu." Then came sixteen men, dressed in uniform, staggering under the weight of an enormous *sambo*, on which rested a gigantic head of Shutendoji, a horned demon with a scarlet complexion. Behind this marched a tall man, bearing a papier-mâché axe, the blade of which was six feet long, and broad in proportion.

As the head was borne past the ward banner, which was erected on a mast opposite the Jewetts, the bearers uttered loud yells, which were re-echoed by the spectators, who appeared to be greatly delighted with the show.

" What does it all mean?" asked Fitz.

Oto smiled, and, shrugging his shoulders, said, —

"It is to honor the memory of Yorimitsu, a warrior who killed Shutendoji, a monster that once devastated the plain of Yedo, and, like all such legendary creatures, used to devour beautiful young girls."

In the rear of the axe-bearer came men in armor, riding white horses, *bozu* in *kago* (litters), more men in armor, umbrella and standard bearers, and a number of carts containing platforms, on which were figures similar to those the travellers had seen at Shimonoseki.

One of the vehicles contained a gigantic figure of Fuku-roku-jin, who was represented with an enormous head and dwarf body, with his right hand raising his bushy right eyebrow, and with his left grasping a long bamboo gnarled at the end.

This figure attracted the attention of Fitz, who whispered to Mrs. Nambo, —

" Who is that old gentleman with a mansard forehead?"

" A what?" she blandly answered.

Oto came to her assistance, and replied, —

"That is the longevity god."

"But why does he have such a big head?" persisted the boy. "Was he afflicted with water on the brain?"

"No," answered Oto; "he was a very wise man, and always thought before he spoke."

"Yes," remarked Johnnie, "that is the reason why he is so much respected. You'll never be like him, Fitz."

"I hope not," was the laughing response. "I don't want a head like the dome of the Capitol at Washington. I bet you he never made unkind remarks to his poor little brother. Wouldn't his head have puzzled the phrenologists?"

FUKU-ROKU-JIN (LONGEVITY GOD).

Their further conversation was cut short by the noise of the drums in the rear of the procession.

When the latter had passed, Miss Kiku clasped her hands palm to palm, and exclaimed,—

"My sakes alive! I want to go to the Golden Pheasant. I haven't a book to read while we are at Hakone! I shall die! The library is not far from here, so please, honorable uncle, let us go that way."

Mr. Nambo gave the runners instructions where to halt, and the party entering their vehicles, were trundled down a side street.

"There is the building," said the young lady, indicating a store, in front of which were some handsome lanterns bearing the sign of the house, and announcements of the latest works; which were also repeated on the walls and short curtains above the doors.

As the *jin-riki-sha* men stopped, Fitz nodded toward a man who carried a comical face in a frame on his back, and said, —

A CIRCULATING LIBRARY.

"Is that an advertisement?"

"No," replied Mrs. Nambo. "He is a pilgrim bearing a representation of a *tengu* head. The *tengu* is a demon said to inhabit unfrequented places."

She would have given a history of the creature, and

otherwise enlightened her hearers, had not Miss Kiku inquired, —

" Honorable aunt, do you wish to procure a novel or two?"

This diverted the old lady's attention, and she descended from her vehicle and entered the building, which was filled with customers and clerks, who were busily engaged receiving and delivering sets of books.

Having selected quite a pile of volumes, they had them checked, then paid the fees and returned to their *jin-riki-sha*, whereupon the party resumed their journey.

The city was dusty, and the air close and hot, so they were glad enough to reach Shinagawa.

" Now for a gallop on the Tokaido," cried Sallie, as they dashed past the railway terminus, which was alive with holiday-seekers just arrived from Yokohama. " Where shall I stop for you?"

"At the Roku-go ferry," said Oto.

Away she went, the *jin-riki-sha* men racing as hard as they could to keep up with her.

" Isn't this jolly!" cried Johnnie, as they passed a *torii* through which could be seen a glimpse of distant Fuji-yama. " Put up the umbrella, Fitz; the sun is fearfully hot."

His brother complied, and they were rattled along at a smart pace, their coolie, a muscular fellow, dressed in neatly patched garments, propelling the vehicle with the greatest ease.

It was a strange sight,[*] two young Americans dressed in Japanese garb, shading their heads with a cotton umbrella, and riding in a curiously shaped vehicle drawn by a man, who, as he ran, thought, —

" What extraordinary creatures these honorable foreigners are, to be sure. They cannot go ten yards without covering

---

[*] *Vide* cover, representing Johnnie and Fitz riding in a *jin-riki-sha*.

their heads with an umbrella. One would think their skulls were made of paper."

At one place a chunky, little, spotted dog with a rudimentary tail, rushed out of a house, and barked defiantly at them, repeating his salutation to each *jin-riki-sha*, and after the last had passed, turning, thoroughly satisfied with his performance, and trotting in-doors.

They overtook Sallie at the ferry, and, when the party had been carried over the stream in the rickety boat, rattled on until they reached Namamugi, where they halted at a celebrated tea-house, and took luncheon.

As they sat and enjoyed the meal, Oto pointed to some trees near the house, and said, —

"It was there the Englishman Richardson lost his life."

"Do tell us all about it," urged Sallie.

"It was a very foolish business," said Oto. "In those days our nobles considered that no one had a right to cross the line of their processions, and the *samurai* always resented such a thing as a deliberate insult to their lords."

"I understand," remarked Johnnie; "just as our people would resent any one attempting to cross a Fourth of July procession."

"Yes, that is a good comparison," answered the Japanese. "Richardson thought he could do as he pleased, and did not consider we had any rights he was bound to respect. He knew that Shimadzo Saburo, a powerful member of the Satsuma clan, was on his way from Yedo (Tokio), notwithstanding which he and some friends, one of whom was a lady, rode out on the Tokaido, and, upon encountering the cortège, deliberately tried to pass through it. The retainers of the noble, deeming the act a premeditated outrage, drew their swords and cut the gentlemen down, but did not harm the lady. Richardson died; and the British bombarded the city of Kagoshima, killed a great number of people, destroyed factories, mills, founderies, and batteries; fired the palace of the Prince, and committed other acts of reprisal. In addition to our losses, we were compelled to pay an indemnity of six hundred and twenty-five thousand dollars."

"Are the English sorry for their barbarous act?" asked Fitz. "Have they ever said anything about returning the money?"

"Not a word," replied Oto, adding, sarcastically, "We had to pay a heavy sum for being civilized."

"So you did," said Johnnie. "Your first experience of foreign nations must have been a particularly unpleasant one."

"Yes," said Fitz, with a chuckle, "they served your countrymen worse than we did you. We only loaded our cannon with a cucumber."

"They were like us," said Sallie, "they did not know you. When they discovered you were the same as themselves, they — they — "

"Made you pay double for everything you bought of them," said Fitz. "I hear that your railway cost about five times as much per mile as it ought to have done."

"We now build our own railroads and steamships," said Oto. "The day has passed for foreign adventurers to make fortunes out of us."

"Boys," said Mr. Nambo, "if you have concluded your discussion we will resume our journey."

For some distance the road lay along the shore of the bay, and was lined with houses and shaded with picturesquely crooked, feathered pitch-pines, some of which formed fantastic arches overhead.

The travellers stopped at Kanagawa, a place famous for

its paper umbrellas, and while resting at a tea-house, Mrs. Nambo recited a poem, which is thus translated,—

> "When it rains, the frogs sing gleefully.
> Happy is he who owns a Kanagawa umbrella."

To which O-Kiku replied,—

> "When the sun shines hotly at mid-day,
> He is fortunate who carries a Tokio *higasa*" (parasol).

"What is that *mon* (crest) on the lantern yonder man is varnishing?" inquired Johnnie, pointing to a workman engaged in the occupation described.

A LANTERN-MAKER.

"That is a *tomoye*," said Mr. Nambo, "a *mon*, formed of three tear-like strokes, painted on lanterns used at *Matsuri*, and on temple drums; it is also imprinted on the edges of roofing tiles."

"What does it mean?" demanded Fitz.

"It is a figure that brings luck to whoever possesses it," observed Mrs. Nambo. "I always carry a paper marked thus in my left sleeve."

"Does it bring you good or bad luck?" said Fitz.

The gentle lady laughed merrily and replied,—

"Sometimes one and sometimes the other;" adding, as she saw Oto approach, "My son, what became of the silver *tomoye* I gave you when you left for America?"

"I — I —" hesitated Oto; then seeing his father was smiling, he said, "Is everything ready? I have paid the bill, and it is time we started."

Fitz chuckled, for he always enjoyed the reference to his comrade's former belief in such things as *tomoye*.

In another moment they were off, Sallie leading on her pony, and the rest of the party in their vehicles, chatting as they rode.

"I admire Oto for his devotion to his mother," said Johnnie. "You ought not to tease him, Fitz."

"Nonsense!" replied the boy. "I think it is fun to hear him respectfully check her when she begins to talk about luck and idols. He is always on the lookout and stops her at the most interesting times. If he did not, we should learn lots about the god-fox, and all those things."

"We know enough," said Johnnie. "I think he is ever so good. Though he does not believe in such things, he is unwilling she should be ridiculed for doing so."

"I never thought of that," answered Fitz, in a reflective tone. "Johnnie, after this I will not try to draw her out. As you say, Oto is a devoted son and a perfect gentleman."

They reached the town of Kanasawa about four o'clock, and put up at the principal *yadoya* (inn), where they partook of an excellent dinner.

That evening, when they were resting in the veranda, and talking over the events of the day, they heard a drumming noise proceeding from a neighboring building.

"Is not that a pretty racket?" tartly remarked their landlady. "It is those absurd Shintos, amusing themselves with their dolls."

"You speak as though you disliked them," observed the Professor.

"Dislike!" she cried. "Why do they plant themselves

right under our noses. We are good Buddhists, and don't wish our children to be corrupted by the Shintos. They are not wanted here."

"Come, boys, we will see what is going on," said Johnnie, rising, and quitting the veranda. Oto and Fitz followed, and they entered a barn-like structure, filled with men dressed in curious robes, and wearing hats adorned with flowers. All of

A SHINTO CEREMONY.

them carried fans, and some held enormous open umbrellas decorated with various figures.

"Look at their pants," whispered Fitz. "They are so loose behind that they have to tie their coats between their limbs, in order to walk."

"Stop!" said Johnnie.

The boys elbowed their way through the crowd toward a

platform surmounted by a canopy under which were some large dolls that were danced to the music of a band, composed of drummers and *samisen* players. As the figures moved, a man, who held a book, sang in a most lugubrious voice.

"What is it all about?" inquired Fitz of one of the worshippers.

"Shinto," mysteriously answered the man.

"Yes; but what does it mean?"

"Shinto," said the fellow.

"I know it is Shinto," persisted the boy. "Tell me what they are doing and why do they do it?"

"I don't know," was the mechanical response. "It does not mean anything. It's Shinto."

The lads watched the puppets awhile, then retired.

When they reached the inn, Fitz related what they had seen, and Mr. Nambo said, —

"Yes, there is nothing in Shintoism. It gives its followers no comfort in this life, and no hope in the future."

"Ah!" sighed his wife, glancing sadly at Oto, "if all the world would only believe in Buddha!" — adding, "My son, to-morrow we will show your friends the beautiful figure of the All-Merciful. I think when you see it, you will forget your new faith and turn to the true path."

The boy did not reply, and Fitz wisely held his peace.

The next morning they rose at daylight, and, after partaking of a light meal, started for the sacred groves of Kamakoura.

## CHAPTER XV.

### THE GREAT BRONZE IMAGE OF BUDDHA.

> Overhead the sky was calm and cloudless;
> Around were the silent woods;
> But neither the calmness of the heavens,
> Nor the stillness of the earth,
> Were as impressive as the serene majesty
> Of Dai-Butsu. — JAPANESE POEM.

AS the sun peeped over the hills of Kamakoura, and flooded the temple-studded valley, a strange procession wended its way along the Kanasawa road in the direction of the Avenue of Hachiman.

First, walked Mr. Nambo, silent and thoughtful, with his head bowed.

Behind him was his wife, who followed with half-closed eyes, murmuring her prayers, every now and again counting off a bead of her rosary, and turning to glance at her recusant son, who was chatting and laughing with his American friends.

At a little distance from the pious lady, came Sallie and O-Kiku, hand in hand, talking merrily, as young girls do, about the patterns of their dresses.

Then came the Professor, Mrs. Jewett, Oto and the boys, in a group; and behind them two servants, with bamboo poles, carrying the hand-valises of the foreigners, and their masters' and mistresses' dressing-cases.

On nearing the spot where the Kanasawa road joined the grand Avenue of Hachiman, which extends from the shore of the bay to the gateway of the temple, they crossed a pretty

## THE GREAT BRONZE IMAGE OF BUDDHA. 265

bridge spanning a brawling stream, and presently came to a place where three *torii* were erected. Two of these stood on the main avenue, and the third at the end of the Kanasawa road. There the travellers encountered a number of pilgrims, moving in the direction of the temple of Hachiman, and saw that they consisted of all classes.

Some of them were dressed in the national style, and wore their hair in the old fashion, in a gun-hammer queue; others allowed their coarse, black locks to grow, and a few wore foreign garb.

The women were all clothed in the becoming native costume, and most of them carried babies on their backs.

The main avenue, like the road from Kanasawa, was bordered with magnificent trees, beyond which could be seen the temple, standing out clearly in the bright sunlight.

"How gratifying it is to see so many pious pilgrims on their way to the sacred place," remarked Mrs. Nambo, as she halted in order to permit Mrs. Jewett to join her. "I feel sure you will all be touched by the majesty of the Dai-Butsu (great statue of Buddha). I have known many people, who came here sceptics, to leave the place converted to the true faith."

Mrs. Nambo never seemed to comprehend that her guests really believed what they professed, and in her kind, motherly way hoped to bring them to what she termed the truth.

Oto, who overheard what his mother said, endeavored to change the subject, but she was full of enthusiasm, and had evidently planned the trip in order to convert her guests.

On their way up the long avenue she chatted alternately with Mrs. Jewett, the Professor, Sallie, and the boys, and was as persistent and sanguine as many of our dear old ladies are over the salvation of the Japanese.

After crossing a bridge, the travellers ascended some steps, and passing the portal, or grand gateway, with its gorgeously colored *Nio* (two kings), and collection of musty sandals, arrived on the first platform, — a large space, enclosed with solid walls of masonry, in which stood many buildings.

On their left were a pagoda and the treasury. The former was a two-storied edifice, bearing a vane called *Kin-do* (nine rings), a solid spiral of copper, surmounted by a gilt design representing the sacred *tama* (jewel, crystal, or pearl), set in the serrated tail of a dragon.

THE PAGODA AND TREASURY OF THE TEMPLE.

The visitors inspected the exteriors of these structures, but were not permitted to see the wealth stored within. A few pilgrims were sauntering about the spot, and the young Americans saw a number of *bozu* who were taking their morning's exercise.

"Stop, Oto," said Mrs. Nambo, as they approached the cistern near the steep flight of steps leading to the temple. "Let me give you a little of this to rinse your mouth and moisten your hands."

Oto, who felt very uncomfortable, and blushed like a girl, shook his head and turned away; noticing which, Fitz advanced and said, —

"Mrs. Nambo, I don't mind taking a drink."

The lady, who a moment before had been full of motherly anxiety for her son, glanced at Fitz's bright, frank face, and smiled; then inserting the wooden dipper in the cistern, handed it to him, saying, —

"Yes, yes, drink, and pour some of the holy liquid over your hands. It may cleanse your mind from its strange belief."

"Oh! you consider that is sacred, do you?" he queried. "Guess I — guess I won't take any — thank you. I'm not thirsty."

This made the spectators laugh, and caused her husband to say, —

"Now, honorable wife, I think you had better leave our honorable guests to do as they please. Purify yourself and follow us."

They climbed the steps, and when they reached the terrace, turned and beheld, at their feet, the grand entrance, the broad avenue, the three *torii*, and the bay of Kamakoura, all of which formed a beautiful panorama; while on their right and left were the wooded hills, dotted here and there with the cells of recluses, who knew nothing, either of the outer world or of modern progress.

They watched this scene for a long time, and would have remained still longer had not Mrs. Nambo said, —

"Do none of our honorable friends desire to go into the temple?"

Of course they said "yes," and, putting off their shoes, followed her, but failed to discover anything of very great interest.

The idols were mean in appearance, and the place what

Fitz termed "stuffy;" so, after a casual inspection, they returned to the open air, leaving their hostess, who said she desired to offer a prayer.

APPROACH TO THE TEMPLE.

On the left of the main porch were some magnificent lanterns of bronze and stone; also a number of cisterns, surmounted by pyramids of buckets — the fire establishment of the temple.

## THE GREAT BRONZE IMAGE OF BUDDHA. 269

While the Professor and rest of the party were viewing the glorious scene, Fitz quietly returned to the temple, where he found Mrs. Nambo, purchasing some slips of paper from a *bozu*. She did not notice the boy's reappearance, and was chatting quite confidentially with the vender of the documents.

"Let me see," she mused, as she counted her purchases. "I have nine for Oto, one for my husband, one for Kiku, and

TERRACE OF THE TEMPLE.

one each for our honored guests from afar. I think I ought to buy more for them, they need praying for."

"I would not waste my money on those infidels," said the *bozu*. "Purchase a package for your son, he sadly requires your prayers."

"Yes, that is wise advice," she murmured. "Ah! my poor boy, his heart has been turned to stone."

During her speech, the *bozu* observed Fitz, and, making a signal to her, whispered, —

"You are watched by one of your honorable guests from afar."

On seeing the boy, she smiled and said, —

"I am going to offer prayers for you."

Fitz chuckled inwardly, but did not reply; so she added, —

"Come and see me make my offerings."

It was a strange sight to watch the trio, — Mrs. Nambo chewing strips of white paper, and gravely throwing them at an idol, which was specked all over with similar missives; the *bozu* regarding her as solemnly as a deacon does a pious person who places a large contribution in the collection plate; and the young American, endeavoring to preserve a serious countenance.

Oto's mother was not a good shot, and the pellets flew wide of the mark.

"Let me try," urged Fitz, checking a rising smile. "Guess I can —"

"No, no," she gently answered. "I must throw them myself."

As he was turning away to indulge in a quiet laugh, he beheld his father, who, regarding him sternly, beckoned him out of the temple.

"Fitz," he said, when they reached the terrace, "remember, though the act of that lady appears absurd, and is idolatrous, your ridicule will not convince her we are in the right. Come away. Of late you have behaved very strangely; what has wrought this change in you?"

The boy looked very penitent, hung his head, and murmured, —

"I think it is the climate, sir! I can't help feeling lively. Did you not tell Mr. Nambo that the air is full of ozone?"

His parent averted his face and bit his lips; the idea of the climate having had such an effect upon his son being quite too much for him.

When the worthy old lady had concluded her devotions, they proceeded to a small temple, from the terrace of which they had a grand view of the surrounding country, the bay of Kamakoura, and the beautiful island of Enoshima.

THE ISLAND OF ENOSHIMA.

"What a magnificent sight!" said the Professor. "Your *bozu* join hands with Nature, and the result is a combination of buildings and natural scenery that is most impressive. No wonder your people love to come hither."

"Would you like to see the great statue at the back of the altar of this temple?" inquired Mrs. Nambo.

"No, thank you," answered Mrs. Jewett. "I think we had better go on to the Dai-Butsu."

"Come this way," said Oto, who was glad enough to avoid the exhibition. "It is quite a little walk to the great statue."

They turned into a winding path, bordered with high shrubs and shaded with aged trees. After walking some distance they came to a bend in the road, on rounding which they suddenly beheld the famous image.

For a moment the entire party remained as though awe-stricken, — Mrs. Nambo sinking on her knees, and bowing her forehead to the ground.

Then Fitz recovered somewhat from his amazement and exclaimed, in a startled voice, —

"Jeminy! what's that?"

"*Namu Amida Butsu!*" murmured Mrs. Nambo.

"Hail, great Buddha!" exclaimed the Professor. "Hail, thou glorious inspiration and majestic creation of a poetic soul!"

"John," whispered his wife, "keep calm!"

"Yes, it is glorious," he continued. "The artist who wrought that must have had his whole soul in his work."

"Guess it was cast, wasn't it?" suggested Fitz, eying the statue critically. "I can see the cracks where the pieces were joined!"

"What repose of feature! How dignified it is!" said Sallie, who did not heed her brother's remark. "Next to Fuji-yama this is the most impressive sight in Japan."

"I wonder how high it is, and how many tons of metal there are in it," said Johnnie to Oto.

"I neither know nor care," was the quick response. "It is, as Sallie says, one of the most impressive sights of my native land."

"Say," whispered Fitz, "why has it a curly head? I never saw one of your countrymen with his hair done up in that fashion."

"Those are not curls," gravely answered Oto. "When

STATUE OF DAI-BUTSU (GREAT BUDDHA).

Buddha was exposed to the broiling sun, the snails clustered on his head and protected the sacred skull."

"I want to know," murmured the irrepressible. "Is that a spit-ball prayer on his forehead?"

"That is the — silver boss or wart," replied Oto, who could scarcely refrain from smiling.

"Oh! Buddha had warts, had he? Why didn't he use — "

"Fitz!" sternly exclaimed the Professor, "remember — "

"I forgot," answered the boy, gazing up at the blue sky. "Isn't it a lovely day, Oto?"

After they had thoroughly enjoyed the sight, the *bozu* in charge of the image advanced toward them, and, bowing, said, —

"Would the honorable visitors from afar like to enter the chapel, and — "

"Yes," replied Oto, "my friends wish to see every part of the Dai-Butsu."

They ascended the steps, and, at the invitation of the guardian, the boys climbed upon the statue, and examined the inscriptions covering the neck and body of the image. These were in very ancient characters that puzzle ordinary scholars to read, and even Mr. Nambo could not decipher them.

While the brothers were thus employed, Oto and his father inspected the bronze altar in front of the idol, and the beautiful lanterns placed at the foot of the pedestal.

Although Mr. Nambo professed to be indifferent to his wife's religion, he stepped upon the block of wood in front of the altar, and poured the contents of a paper of incense into the censer, from which presently rose a blue smoke that floated hither and thither on the still air.

"Hi, Sallie!" cried Fitz, "won't you come up here?"

"I am worshipping from afar," answered the girl. "This is indeed a wonderful statue!"

## THE GREAT BRONZE IMAGE OF BUDDHA. 275

The boys descended from their elevation, and followed the *bozu* into a little chapel in the base of the figure.

At first they could scarcely see anything, though when their eyes became accustomed to the gloom, they beheld an altar lighted from an aperture away up in the neck-folds of Buddha's robe.

At high noon the sun, shining down the interior of the figure, illuminates the altar in a brilliant manner; however, at the time the boys visited the place, the light was only sufficient to partly reveal the objects in the chapel.

While the young Americans were inspecting the decorations, the *bozu* was opening a case that he had drawn from a recess under the altar. He was a wizen-faced, pithecoid individual, with ferret-like eyes, and a furtive manner that greatly amused Fitz, who, noticing the man's act, said in English, —

"What is he about?"

"Unpacking something," replied Johnnie.

The object of their remark knelt by the box, tore off a layer of straw covering its contents, and drawing forth a bottle, said in a confidential tone, —

"Only fifty *sen*."

"What is it — a relic?" demanded Fitz, who by the dim light could not clearly distinguish the object. "We are not Buddhists."

"It is *mugi-saké* (beer)," whispered the *bozu*.

"What?" cried Johnnie.

"*Bee-ah!*" replied the man, smiling hideously. "You English people always ask for it when you come here. Only fifty *sen*."

The lads could scarcely believe the evidence of their ears. When he repeated his offer, and stripping off the paper, exhibited the highly colored label, Johnnie said, —

"My friend, we are Americans. We ca drinking beer."

"Americans?" cried the *bozu*, grinning more diabolically than before, and rapidly putting the bottle back into the case. "Oh — I have something that will suit you better. Wait for a moment."

Away he went, leaving the amazed boys wondering what he was going to show them.

"Guess he has some pork and beans cooking in his den," murmured Fitz. "He's a regular Yankee."

In a few moments back came the *bozu*, carrying a large bag, which he unceremoniously dumped upon the altar.

"I have some pieces of the Dai-Butsu here," he whispered, as though afraid of being overheard by the pilgrims, who were arriving in great numbers. "You can have fragments of the snails or of the robe — only one *yen* each —"

"We are not buying old metal to-day," answered Fitz. "Here is a *yen* for your kindness, but we do not want any specimens. *Sayonara* (farewell)."

They rejoined their friends, and Fitz told his father of their adventure, when the Professor smiled and said, —

"I suppose the demand has produced the supply. Some Englishmen cannot visit such a spot as this without asking for beer, and our countrymen have a weakness for relics."

"You were wise not to purchase any of the latter," observed Mr. Nambo. "That *bozu* sells tons of pieces of the Dai-Butsu in a year. It is a source of revenue."

After they had taken a farewell look at the majestic figure, which had quite enchanted the Professor, Mrs. Jewett, and Sallie, they retired, and made the best of their way toward the Grand Avenue.

They had planned to visit the Island of Enoshima, then hire *jin-riki-sha* and *kago* and go up to Hakone, where they intended to stay with one of Mr. Nambo's relatives, who had sent a most pressing invitation to the entire party.

"I shall never think of Japan without remembering the Dai-Butsu," said Sallie.

"And I shall never think of the Dai-Butsu without remembering that comical *bozu*," laughingly observed Johnnie. "He has missed his vocation — he ought to be driving a peddler's cart."

"We can obtain *jin-riki-sha* here," said Oto, as they reached a tea-house on the Avenue. "It is four miles to Enoshima, and we shall have plenty of walking to do after we get there."

They refreshed themselves, and, after resting awhile, entered the vehicles, and were trundled down the pilgrim-crowded avenue, and across the sand spit that unites the mainland to the sacred island.

On reaching the latter, their runners halted, and the travellers alighted, passed beneath a *torii*, and ascended the stair-like street, on each side of which were shops filled with curiosities; among them being the so-called pencil-coral, that looks like plumes of spun glass, but is in reality the legs of once living organisms of the sponge tribe. They also saw quantities of artificial flowers made of shells, corals, conchs, and sea-ferns; Enoshima being famous for its marine curiosities.

Every other house was a hotel, and nearly all the buildings bore this sign —

PLEASANT ACCOMMODATIONS FOR PILGRIMS.

Mr. Nambo conducted them to a comfortable inn, and as soon as they had dined, the landlord took them into the rear yard of the establishment and showed them some gigantic crabs, with shells two feet across, and claws six feet in length

"I do not think you can beat those," slyly observed Oto, as Fitz prodded the monsters with a bamboo.

"Pooh!" returned the boy; "I have seen crabs among the Cromlech rocks that you could not get into a barrel."

"Oh, Fitz Jewett!" exclaimed his sister; "what a dreadful story! You never saw one there that was too large to go into a barrel."

"I did not say anything of the kind," he answered with a chuckle. "I said they wouldn't go into a barrel, — more they would. You couldn't get them to, anyhow."

The young Americans thoroughly explored Enoshima, viewed the temple of Benten, and the cave on the shore, where the white dragons were said to have once made their home, and where now, at high tide, enormous cuttle-fish sometimes lurk and prey upon the fishermen. The boys saw everything, and asked the guide so many questions that he was glad when night came, and they returned to their hotel.

Enoshima, the island Benten is supposed to have raised from the sea after she drove the dragons out of the marshes of Yedo Bay, is the favorite resort of pilgrims, who pray at her shrine, and enjoy the lovely scenery.

The Jewett party spent the next morning at the inn, then started for Lake Hakone. On their way they crossed many streams, and passed through scenery that reminded them of the White Mountains.

As they halted at Odawara to change from *jin-riki-sha* to *kago* (litters), Fitz, who was watching a man fastening a tablet to the door-post of a house, said to Oto, —

"What is that notice about?"

"Do you not know?" replied his friend. "The government requires every householder to place over his door a list of the names, ages, and occupations of all persons living under the roof, and severely punishes any one who, on the arrival or

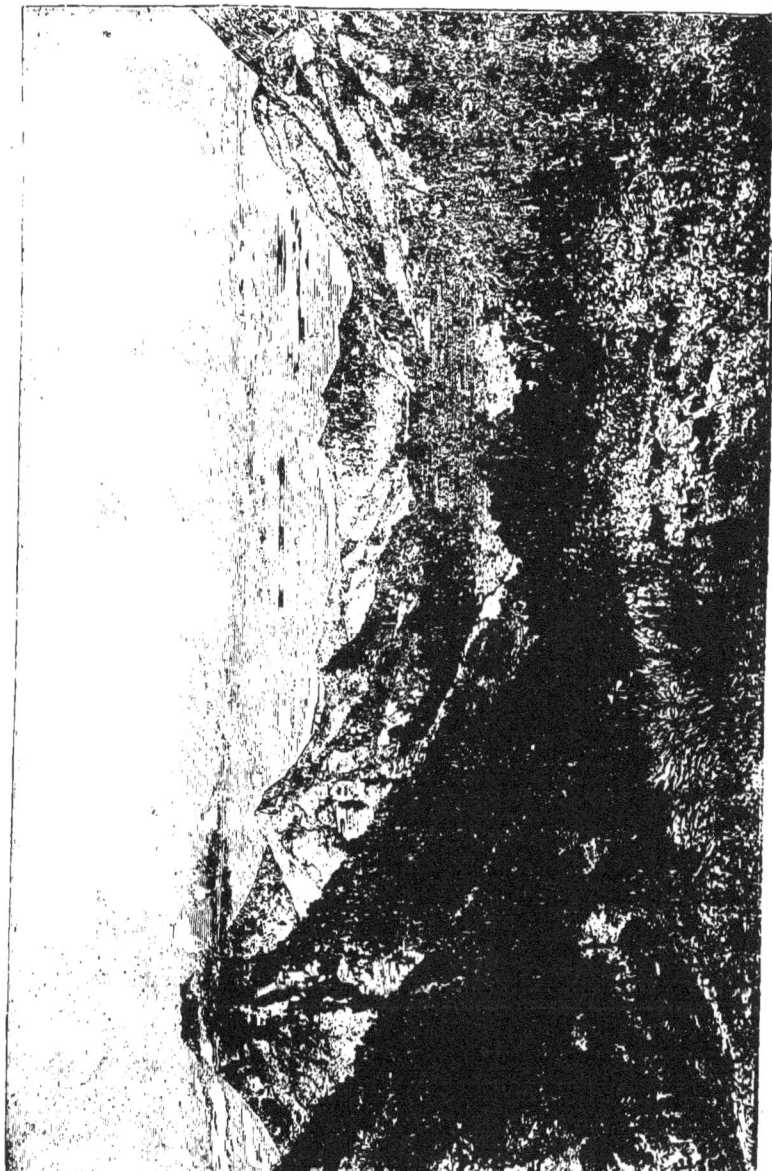

VIEW OF LAKE HAKONE.

departure of a guest, fails to correct the record. We have such a tablet on the outside of our house, and you will find it on every building, except the residences of his Majesty the Mikado, and of high officials."

"But what good is it?" demanded Fitz.

"It is exceedingly useful," answered Oto. "It facilitates the taking of the census, and acts as a check upon criminals, who find it impossible to seclude themselves long from the officers of justice. It would be an excellent plan for you to adopt in the States."

"We are a free people," laughingly answered the boy. "Our citizens would not submit to such a thing."

On the last day of September they arrived at their destination, and were welcomed by Mr. Ito, who had a charming residence overlooking Lake Hakone, and who proved to be a most accomplished, genial gentleman.

That evening they assembled on the veranda of the dwelling, where they sat and watched the white sails drifting to and fro on the bosom of the lake, and beheld, across the range, the purple cone of cloud-crested Fuji-yama.

"How many feet is that above the level of the sea?" asked Johnnie of Oto, who was dreamily regarding the beautiful scenery.

"About thirteen thousand," was the drowsy reply. "Is it not sufficient that the view is lovely, without troubling one's mind as to the height of the mountain?"

"Oh, you are a thorough Japanese," said Johnnie.

"And you are a thorough American," answered his friend. "I think this place is as near to Paradise as we poor mortals shall ever get."

## CHAPTER XVI.

**JAPANESE NEW YEAR FESTIVITIES.**

> As soon as it is daybreak
> The housemaid goes to the well,
> And, grasping the rope, cries,
> " Turn easily, gentle wheel,
> For I am now dipping
> The water of congratulation
> For the New Year!" — JAPANESE POEM.

ONE cold, snowy morning in December, Fitz was looking out of the bay-window of a foreign-built house in the official quarter of Tokio. Near him was Johnnie, seated at a table studying, and on the other side of the apartment Sallie was furiously driving a sewing-machine.

A great change had taken place in their arrangements, as, since September, their father had temporarily accepted the chemical chair in the Imperial College, and they had hired a house and furnished some of the rooms in the American fashion.

Fitz, who was in his ordinary garb, stood watching a *jin-riki-sha* man who had taken up his position against the fence on the opposite side of the road, and, with his hands thrust into his sleeves, was hugging himself in a manner peculiar to the Japanese.

" *Samui, samui* (cold, cold)!" muttered the half-frozen coolie.

The boy of course could not hear this, but interpreted the motion of the man's lips, and echoed, —

" *Samui!* Yes, you are right. Say, Johnnie, Oto is here,

JIN-RIKI-SHA MAN.

he has just entered the porch. His *kuruma* (another name for *jin-riki-sha*) man is standing under the lee of the fence, and shivering like a sick cat."

In a few moments Oto, dressed in American costume, entered the room, and, after saluting his friends, seated himself by the stove, and exclaimed, —

"You are delightfully warm in here. I'm chilled to the marrow."

"How long will this cold spell last?" inquired Sallie, ceasing her occupation, and advancing toward him. "It is a heavy fall of snow for Tokio, is it not?"

"Ye — ye — yes," he answered, warming his blue-looking fingers. "We have not had such a blessing — ugh — for twenty years. Thank goodness, the snow is melting fast, and will probably all be gone by New Year's day. By the way, Sallie, I have come to invite you and the boys to spend the holidays with us. My father and mother have sent you a written invitation," handing her a note. "O-Kiku is coming to our house, and we are going to keep the New Year in the old fashion."

"I have no doubt mamma and papa will let us go," said the young lady. "I hope your honorable parents are enjoying good health."

While they were chatting, the Professor passed the window. He was smiling, and as usual, muffled in his long cloak, and wore a broad-brimmed felt hat, by which he was becoming known all over Tokio.

On noticing Oto, he nodded, and when he joined the group, said,—

"Well, doctor, how do you do, and how are your honorable parents?"

"What is amusing you, sir?" asked Fitz, as he watched his father's face.

"Oh, nothing," replied the Professor. "Just now, when I was leaving the college gate, I saw a *bozu*, waiting for me, and near him a bald-headed boy, watching the *bozu*. As I approached the man, he dropped on his knees, and, after bowing repeatedly, cried,—

"'Great foreign lady, will you give me a plaster to cure my cough?'

"The boy listened with a mocking expression, then raising his hands derisively, ran past me, crying,—

"'Hai! Hai! here's a good joke! The old *bozu* can't cure himself, and is obliged to ask the aid of that foreign lady.'"

"They took you for Mrs. Dr. Crispman," laughingly observed Oto.

"Oh, papa, do have your hair cut," said Sallie. "The people will not believe you are a gentleman."

"Well, papa is," said Fitz. "There is no mistake about that."

"Well, well, I'll have my hair cut by machinery, the same as Oto does," merrily replied the Professor, alluding to the young doctor's closely cropped head. "Anything to please you, daughter."

When he had read Mr. Nambo's letter, he said,—

"I guess you young folks can go. There is to be a ball at the house of the Minister for Foreign Affairs, a review of the troops, and lots of gay doings, but you can attend them all. How many days will your holiday last, Oto?"

"From the first to the fifteenth," he replied. "I cannot remain at home over the third,"— adding naïvely, "the patients require the same attendance during a *matsuri* as at any other time."

It was finally agreed that the young people should visit Mr. and Mrs. Nambo from the last day of the old year to the third of the new, then return home and enjoy the modern features of the great holiday.

Mrs. Jewett, who was of course consulted, thought this would be the wisest plan, so a letter of acceptance was written, and handed to Oto, who went off to the hospital, delighted with the idea of once more enjoying a good time with his old friends.

The snow rapidly vanished, and on the last day of the year the air of Tokio was mild and balmy.

"Come, Sallie," shouted Fitz, that afternoon, as they entered their *jin-riki-sha*, "we are ready! Johnnie says we ought to take a ride about the city, and see the preparations for the holiday."

The young lady soon made her appearance, and they set out.

## JAPANESE NEW YEAR FESTIVITIES.

Modern Tokio, the official portion of the city where the houses are built of brick and stone, was alive with soldiers, foreigners, and natives in American costume. Flags of all nations were fluttering in the breeze, and when the young people looked at the stores, gas lamps and telegraph wires, they could scarcely believe they were in the land of the Rising Sun; however, after they left that part of the city, and entered

MOB BEFORE A SAKÉ SHOP.

a district untouched by the hand of the reformer, everything was different.

"What is that crowd shouting about?" asked Fitz, as their vehicles were stopped by a throng of yelling servants, most of whom carried tubs, bottles or buckets. "Is there a fire any where?"

"No," answered one of the *jin-riki-sha* men; "this is the day the *saké* dealers tap the new liquor. Those people are after their supply for the holidays. That shop is behindhand in opening its doors, and the servants are indignant at the delay."

The proprietor of the establishment and some of his assistants came out on the roof of the porch, and shouted to the people to be patient.

EMBOSSING VISITING-CARDS.

"What does he say?" asked Sallie.

"L i s t e n," said Fitz.

The *saké* dealer leaned over the rail and said, in a loud voice, —

"Good friends! good friends! Wait a few moments. The *bozu* says my *saké* must not be tapped until the sun sets. Now, you surely do not want to bring misfortune on yourselves by compelling me to serve it before the auspicious moment arrives."

"Oh, go to!" shouted an unbeliever in the crowd. "Give the *bozu* a bottle, and send him back to the temple."

"It's a fact!" yelled an employé, who stood behind the proprietor and endeavored to calm the crowd by waving a dipper. "Wait until the lucky moment arrives."

Just then the *jin-riki-sha* men noticed an opening in the assembly, and, availing themselves of it, were soon clear of the noisy throng.

During their tour of inspection, the Jewetts passed many shops in which artists were preparing the ornamental visiting-cards used during the festivities. These were embossed with various patterns, by being passed through a wooden machine that somewhat resembled a clothes-wringer. Millions of such strips of paper are annually manufactured, and are as much sought after as our Christmas cards.

It was quite late before the young Americans concluded their round, and the streets were beginning to be densely

WELCOMING THE NEW RICE.

crowded with people making holiday purchases. Most of them carried lanterns, and appeared in the best possible humor.

"All Tokio is having a good time," said Johnnie, as they halted before a rice warehouse. "I wonder what those coolies with the long lanterns are yelling about?"

"They are welcoming the new rice," said one of the runners. "Most of them are house-servants out for a frolic. They assemble in front of the stores of merchants from whom their masters have, during the year, purchased rice. Then they shout, raise their lanterns, clap their hands, and repeat their cry, which attracts the proprietors, who invite the men in and treat them to *saké.*"

"What is that double straw cornucopia for?" asked Sallie.

"It means that new rice is for sale within," replied the man.

"I have seen enough of this," said Fitz. "Come, let us go on to Mr. Nambo's; he will think we are lost."

On reaching the entrance to their friend's estate, they found a green bamboo planted on one side, and a young pine-tree on the other; the trees being connected by a rope of straw.

"Now, we are going to see something of the olden customs," said Johnnie, as they heard the shouts of the *mochi*-makers in the courtyard. "I tell you, this is like old times, when the Shogun was the master of Yedo."

The guests were welcomed by their host, hostess, and O-Kiku, and when the ladies had retired the boys followed Mr. Nambo into the courtyard to see the *mochi*-makers.

*Mochi* is a sweet dough made in a peculiar manner by beating rice flour and sugar in an enormous wooden mortar. It is a luxury consumed in large quantities during the New Year festivities, and is eaten either uncooked, steamed, or fried. Years ago the *mochi*-makers went from house to house, and were a source of great amusement to the children. Now the delicacy is manufactured at large establishments.

Although there were only seven men in the party employed by Mr. Nambo, they made as much noise as seventy ordinary servants. All of them were stripped to the waist, had towels tied about their heads, and were yelling as though their lives depended upon their cries.

The rice-flour and sugar were slightly moistened, and pounded in a mortar formed of the section of a trunk of a tree; the stout pestle being provided with a short handle. The operators often removed the dough from the vessel and threw it back with a dull thud.

In the centre of the courtyard was a portable furnace,

MOCHI-MAKERS.

formed of fire-clay, surmounted by a copper boiler, and a steamer in which the prepared dough was being cooked.

*Mochi* is to a Japanese what turkey and mince pies are to an American, and roast beef and plum pudding are to an Englishman — a sign of festivity.

When the boys re-entered the house, they noticed a gentleman seated in the corridor, writing by the light of a little lamp. On his right hand stood a vase filled with iris leaves, round the base of which were inserted the heads of some dried sardines stuck in cleft sticks. Upon a raised recess was a *sambo* filled with roasted chestnuts, *gaya* (peanuts), bunches of *noshi* (dried sea-weed), and a cup of raw rice; the whole being decorated with evergreens, ferns, and branches of pine.

The stranger was well-dressed, and wore American eye-glasses, that gave his face a peculiar appearance.

A POET AT WORK.

"He is a professional poet whom I have engaged to write my New Year's cards," whispered the host. "Shohei is quite a celebrated man. Let me present him to you."

The boys advanced, and were introduced; then the poet, after much bowing and sucking in of his breath, took a sheet of paper and wrote, in large characters, down the centre,—

"*Omereto*" (congratulations), adding, on the left side, in a beautiful, flowing hand, a poem, which may be thus translated, —

> "During the past year
> I have received many kindnesses from you,
> And wish that the same may be repeated
> During the coming year."

He signed, stamped, and folded this, then handed it to Fitz.

"Any charge?" whispered the boy, fumbling for his purse.

"No, no," breathed Mr. Nambo. "I pay him for everything he does."

They left the writer hard at work, and entered their host's private room, where they saw many new *kakemono* (hanging pictures), and Mr. Nambo said, —

"I keep these in my *kura*" (fire-proof store-house), a structure, built behind the houses of the wealthy, in which are deposited the treasures of the family — money, dresses, works of art, etc.

"I see," said Johnnie. "You change your house decorations every now and then, and don't put all your pictures on your walls at once, as we do."

The old gentleman bowed and replied, —

"We like to display a few choice paintings at a time, we thus have an opportunity to fully examine them and appreciate their beauties. If we had them always before our eyes, they would soon cease to charm us."

"That is sensible," murmured Fitz. "Too much familiarity begets contempt."

"May we come in?" asked Mrs. Nambo.

"Yes, honorable wife," replied her husband. "I was about to send for you and our honorable young lady guests."

"What does that represent?" said Johnnie, as Mrs. Nambo, Sallie and O-Kiku joined them. "Is it not a picture of yourself and a friend?"

"Ah!" sighed their host. "That depicts me in my old

ceremonial dress, receiving a guest on New Year's day. The other gentleman is my cousin. You see he has just placed his present on the *sambo*, before me, and I am acknowledging his respectful congratulations."

"I suppose you sucked in your breath considerably," said Fitz. "Why do you do that?"

NEW YEAR'S PRESENTS.

"Why do you raise your hat to a lady?" demanded Mr. Nambo.

"It is our custom," was the reply.

"Audibly drawing in the breath is our way of expressing respect," quietly returned their friend.

"Is that a lobster perched upon a loaf, on the *sambo* behind your cousin?" said Sallie.

"Yes," replied their host. "I shall have such a symbol, o-morrow, on the *tokonoma* of this room. That represents a *sambo*, on which are two cakes of *mo chi*, surmounted by a boiled lobster, — the red color of which signifies luck that lasts. It is a token of continued happiness."

"Why do you have a poet to write your cards?" demanded Fitz.

"Why do you have your cards printed?" said O-Kiku.

"To save us the trouble of writing them," said the boy.

Mr. Nambo smiled and remarked, —

"Now you know why I employ a poet."

Fitz laughed, and going close to another *kakemono*, said, —

"What does that mean? Is it not a hare bowing and trembling before a wild boar?"

THE DAIMIO AND HATAMOTO.

"Yes," nodded Mr. Nambo. "That is a caricature directed against the old order of things. It represents a *hatamoto* (yeoman farmer) asking for justice at the hands of a *daimio*. I keep it on account of the excellence of the drawing."

"I suppose the great lords used to bully the yeoman farmers," bluntly observed Fitz. "I see, it is something like a poor Irish peasant imploring his haughty landlord to reduce his rent."

"I do not understand your meaning," said Mr. Nambo.

Sallie explained, and when their host had mastered the facts of the case, he said, —

"All that sort of thing is abolished now."
"Not in Ireland," said Fitz.
"My gracious! What is this about?" cried Sallie, pointing to a *kakemono* representing a man throwing something at two hideous demons, while in the background Dai-koku and Yebisu were enjoying a bowl of hot *saké*

THE CEREMONY OF ONIWA SOTO.

"Ah!" exclaimed the old gentleman. "That is a picture of a ceremony we call *Oniwa soto* (expelling the demons). You must know that to-day is termed *Toshi koshi* (passing away of the year). I performed a similar ceremony this evening, just before you arrived."

"Please, tell us all about it," said Sallie.

Mr. Nambo smiled and continued, —

"I roasted some beans, mixed them with some broken charcoal, brick and potsherd, and put the mixture in a rice masu (two-quart measure), then I dressed myself in my old ceremonial robes, took a *sambo* in my left hand, placed the *masu* on it and bade my youngest male servant follow me with a broom. We first entered my sleeping-room and closed the door to within an inch or so, then I threw a handful of the broken stuff to the ceiling and cried, '*Fukuwa uchi oniwa soto.*' (Good fortune come in, bad go out)."

"What jolly fun!" exclaimed Fitz. "Well?"

"The ceremony is not a joke," gently observed Mrs. Nambo.

"Honorable wife," said her husband, "it no doubt appears amusing to our honorable guests. You forget they do not observe the ceremony of *Oniwa soto.*"

"Please, go on," urged Sallie. "Do not mind what my brother says. He sees fun in everything. I think your ceremonies are perfectly charming."

Mr. Nambo bowed, sucked in his breath, and continued,—

"After I had made the adjuration, my servant shouted: '*Gomotomu osaye mashu.*' (You are quite right). Saying which, he slapped his broom on the floor as though driving out the demons. When I had cried and he answered me thrice, we retired to the next room, carefully closing the door of my chamber behind us. We visited each apartment and repeated the ceremony, then I threw what remained in the *masu* at the demons who were skulking about the veranda."

"Was old Mitsu-ro one of them?" inquired Fitz.

"My honorable husband threw the missives at the *oni* (imps) that always gather about a house during times of festivities," quietly observed Mrs. Nambo. "We put a fringe of pine branches and straw all round the eaves of the veranda to keep away those dreadful things. They are invisible."

"I want to know!" murmured the boy.

"Yes, and we place dried sardines' heads in cleft sticks in each entry," continued the lady.

"You saw those *shaga* (iris) leaves and other symbols in the vase near the poet? Well, they both mean the same thing."

"How comical!" muttered Fitz. "I don't think the fish-heads smell nice."

"Hush!" whispered Sallie. "I consider all these customs just splendid."

"But what do they signify?" demanded the unabashed boy.

"That spring is near," answered their hostess. "These symbols were formerly used some months later, when the almanac denoted that spring had begun, which was also about the time of our New Year's day. Now the government has abolished the old way of reckoning time, and our ancient customs and modern dates are all mixed up. Properly speaking, we should not decorate our houses with the iris and sardine-heads until winter has departed. Ah!" sighing, "everything is in a terrible muddle."

"Is this anything to do with the New Year?" inquired Sallie, indicating a picture which represented a lady and her daughter at a *tokonoma*, filled with dolls and vases containing dwarf and grotesque trees.

"That is a painting of our Little Girls' Day," answered Mrs. Nambo. "It occurs on the third of March."

"It is very much like your Santa Claus festival," said O-Kiku. "It depicts a mother and her eldest daughter arranging the family dolls and the gifts for the little ones, on the *tokonoma*, the back of which is decorated with the red sun of Japan. This is done after the young children are in bed. The dolls, which represent great personages, are only brought out once a year and are highly prized by us. I like to dress the *tokonoma* for my little sisters."

"I did not know you had any sisters," said Fitz.

"Oh, yes!" was the smiling reply. "I have three. You will see them when you honor us with a visit. We live at Nikko, up in the mountains, where the Shoguns are buried."

THE LITTLE GIRLS' FESTIVAL.

"In a cemetery?" he asked. "Is it not awfully gloomy there?"

O-Kiku laughed merrily, and replied,—

"No, it is a lovely spot. We have a very old saying: 'No one who has not seen Nikko (sunny splendor) should use the word *Kekko* (beautiful, grand, delightful). It is a charming place. You should visit it and see the falls of Kiri-furi (falling mist) and Kegon (the morning's mirror) on Lake Chiuzenjii, and the golden light illuminating Nantaizan. At Nikko we have the most glorious scenery and the grandest trees in Japan. Sallie has promised to spend next summer with me."

They laughed and chatted until Oto arrived, when he proposed they should go to his room and play *Mon* (crests).

"I know that game," said Fitz. "It is just first-class. We have it in the States, and Sallie and I have played it many a time."

"Yes, and Cash (*cho-moku*) too," said the young lady. "We are indebted to Japan for some of our best games."

"Do you know one we call *Akambo* (red baby)?" inquired O-Kiku. "It is a favorite with our young folks."

"You mean the one played with five counters on a big, red face," said Johnnie. "Oh! we know that. All those games are published in America."

"Then you owe us something," laughingly answered O-Kiku.

"Yes," nodded the boy, "but we taught your students how to play base-ball, and eat ice-cream."

"Oto," said his cousin," you never ate it, did you?"

The young doctor laughed.

"My son never drank milk or ate cream, I am certain," said Mrs. Nambo.

Again Oto indulged in a chuckle.

"Of course he did," said Fitz. "Everybody in the States does."

"I suppose I may as well own up," merrily observed the culprit. "I am afraid it will shock my honorable mother, but the truth is, I not only drank milk, and ate ice-cream, but, saddest of all, partook of butter three times a day, and — am really fond of cheese."

Mrs. Nambo sighed, and regarding him sorrowfully, said, —

"Then no wonder you changed your religion. Doctor

Choan assures me all the articles you have named affect the brain. They are slow poisons."

"Very slow," murmured the amused Fitz. "They haven't killed him yet."

"Can you play *Go* (five)?" asked O-Kiku, after they had enjoyed several of the games before described.

"Do you mean Go-bang?" inquired Johnnie.

"No, *Go*," she said. "*Ban* is the board on which we play. We have no such game as Go-bang."

"That is what we call it," said Fitz.

"Yes, and vulgarize the proper name," returned Sallie. "I never called it so."

"*Go* is the oldest game we have," observed O-Kiku. "It is very difficult to master the correct rules."

"I learnt it in five minutes," said Fitz. "We do not bother ourselves about rules; we try to get five men of a color in a line, then shout Go-bang, and our opponent is —— banged."

"That is not *Go*," proudly answered the young lady. "Ours is a very intricate affair, and is played with the greatest care."

"Yes," said Oto, "in the old time, if an outsider interfered in a game of *Go*, the players cut off his head and placed it in a receptacle, provided for that purpose, under the *ban*"

"You don't say!" cried Fitz. "Johnnie would soon have lost his head. He always interfered when Sallie and I played Go-bang."

They laughed, joked, and amused themselves until midnight, when they retired to their rooms.

At daybreak the young Americans were awakened by the news-venders on the avenue, who were chanting a novel kind of poem, sold only during the holidays.

These men supply their customers with anything from a New-Year's card to a comic song, and when they do not have the poem required, will pass some other off on their patrons, just as our newsboys will sell a chance customer an old number of a paper.

As the boys were listening to the noises, Oto shouted from the next room, —

"*Omereto* (congratulations)! *Shin-nen kei ga* (New Year's joyous welcome)!"

In another moment he was in their apartment, and down on his hands and knees, bowing in the old Japanese fashion.

SONG-SELLERS ON THE STREET.

Johnnie and Fitz replied in the same way, and sucked in their breath, laughing as they did so, and knocking their foreheads on the floor.

The lads then proceeded to the entrance of Mr. Nambo's room, repeated the ceremony, and presented him with cards of congratulation, and the gifts they had brought for the occasion.

"Ah! this reminds me of my young days," sighed the old gentleman. "Do you not like our way of saluting?"

"Well, I can't say I do," replied Fitz. "I dislike to drive tacks with my forehead."

"Do what?" inquired their host.

"He means the act is like driving nails into a carpet," answered Oto. "In America the floors are covered with woollen cloths kept in place by small nails driven along the edges. Hence Fitz's reference to driving tacks."

Mr. Nambo smiled, though he evidently did not appreciate the joke.

"I like to shake hands," said Johnnie, "to give a friend a good grip — it means something."

"And you, Oto?" asked Mr. Nambo.

"I own I prefer the American fashion," answered his son. "The fact is, honorable father, when dressed in foreign garb, one cannot very well perform the respectful salutation.

"Ah!" exclaimed his parent. "You will never forget what you learned in the United States."

"We hope not," thought the young Americans.

After they had conversed awhile, they went to Mrs. Nambo's room, and paid their respects to her and the young ladies.

Sallie was dressed in Japanese costume, and Kiku in American, both looking quite charming.

While they were complimenting each other, old Mitsu-ro entered, and falling upon her hands and knees, bowed her head, and presented Oto with a package, after which she saluted the boys, her mistress, and the young ladies.

As she rose, they heard a shout from the kitchen, and a child's voice, crying, —

"Hai! hai! hai!"

"It is that young imp, Taro, Izakura's son," angrily remarked Mitsu-ro. "He is always making a noise about something."

"Suppose we go and ascertain the cause of his excitement?" said Oto.

Away went the boys, who, on arriving in the kitchen, beheld a most amusing sight.

Izakura, the cook, had purchased a mask, representing the face of a *tengu* (long-nosed demon), and had donned it in order to surprise his boy, instead of doing which he had scared his wife, who was squatting on the floor with outstretched hands, yelling, —

"*Sari, sari*, (go away — go away)." *

Izakura extended his arms and danced in a grotesque fashion, while his son, who was lying on the floor, kicked his feet in the air, pointed at him gleefully, and shouted, —

"*Toki-no-koye!*" (equivalent to hurrah).

"Ugh!" shrieked the woman, whose hair fairly bristled.

"Hello!" cried Fitz. "What is this?"

Izakura removed the mask and handed it to his delighted son, then fell upon his hands and knees, and bowing his face to the floor, said, —

"Honorable master and guests, I humbly wish you the congratulations of the New Year."

The boy laid aside his present and followed his father's example, and the woman did the same.

"What were you doing?" demanded Oto.

"Honorable master," said Izakura, rising and standing with his head inclined respectfully, "I bought that mask for my son, and, thinking to astonish him, put it on, when my silly wife pretended to be alarmed."

"Pretended!" snapped the woman. "I thought you had fallen and hurt your beautiful nose. I'm not frightened by a *tengu* mask, — the likeness was what alarmed me."

Fitz roared, and Izakura darted a reproachful glance at his better half, then, after listening a moment to a noise outside, said, —

"Honorable master, there are the *Etas* (beggars); would you like to witness their capers?"

---

\* *Vide* illustration on paper cover

# JAPANESE NEW YEAR FESTIVITIES.

The lads went into the veranda, and, standing behind the bamboo shade that screened the entrance to the kitchen, saw two men, wearing tall, conical hats of rushes, decorated with streamers of paper, who were dancing to the sound of sticks, which they struck together.

They performed some clumsy antics, and shouted vigorously, stopping every now and then to utter calf-like bleats.

"Why do they wear aprons?" asked Johnnie.

ETA DANCERS.

"I do not know," answered Oto. "Formerly those creatures were considered lower than the animals, and when they intruded on private premises, the servants used to kill them as they would wild beasts. Now they are, in the eyes of the law, regarded as good as any one."

After the Etas had given an exhibition of their agility, and demonstrated the power of their lungs, Izakura threw them a *sen*, and they went off laughing, and making saucy remarks about the appearance of the young Americans.

"Ah!" said Oto. "That comes of placing beggars upon an

equality with decent people. I would have kept them in their proper place, and only emancipated those who deserved it. They are impertinent because they are ignorant."

"Just like our vagabond negroes," said Fitz. "I'm glad they are free. It does not do to oppress any body of men because some of their number are too talkative."

"Just so," slyly answered Johnnie. "If that were so we should be punished for your chatter."

His brother made a grimace, and laughingly retorted,—
"You mean my eloquence."

They returned to Oto's room, and about eight o'clock were summoned to a breakfast served in the old style, at the conclusion of which visitors began to arrive.

Some of the callers were dressed in the national garb, but the majority of the gentlemen wore black dress-suits, and shirts with frilled bosoms, carried tall, black hats, and were accompanied by their wives, costumed in the latest Parisian fashion.

In the middle of the day the boys slipped off, and took a stroll about the city.

"The Tokians have gone mad," said Fitz, as they paused to watch the crowd on Little Monkey Street.

Children were everywhere, — on the pavement, in their nurse's arms and on their backs, flying kites, playing horse, and, what Fitz termed, "playing Cain," in which amusement they were joined by their elders.

A man, wearing a bearded mask and a conical hat, and who blew a brass instrument resembling a speaking-trumpet, and sounding like a bagpipe, was encased in a frame-work, made to represent a pony, the legs of which dangled in a very amusing manner. He gambolled among the crowd, and knocked over the youngsters right and left, notwithstanding which nobody interfered with him, and he continued his mad career, followed by an admiring party. In his evolutions he floored a

STREETS OF TOKIO. NEW YEAR'S AFTERNOON.

lad, who was carrying a toy representing a fox, dressed in man's clothes, and a fat *bozu*, attached to the stick of a tiny umbrella. As this flew out of his hand he began to howl,—

"Oh, my god-fox!—Oh, my god-fox!"

"Hi!" cried his brother, rushing in front of the man and extending his hands. "Don't you damage Sabro's god-fox."

In another instant the speaker was on top of his brother. Seeing this, a boy, who was assisting a comrade to rig a square kite, decorated with a painting of a flying stork, cried,—

"Yeh! Why didn't you fellows keep out of the way? Take your god-fox indoors if you don't want it broken."

Some of the females wore blue cotton hoods, thickly wadded to keep their ears warm, while others went bare-headed, as though indifferent to the keenness of the frosty air.

Women and men were shouting and dancing, and the storekeepers were doing a rousing trade in *saké* and sweetmeats.

Almost every house was dressed with green bamboos or branches of pine, and had strings of straw and sprigs of pine stretched along the eaves.

Johnnie complained that the noise gave him a headache, so Oto proposed they should return home.

Just outside the house they met Oto's old schoolmaster and his wife, who were dressed in American costume.

The gentleman bowed and said "*Omereto*," and the lady, after shaking hands with them, remarked in English,—

"I Wash you a hop-eye nose-ears."

Fitz would have commented on this had not Johnnie checked him and complimented the lady upon her knowledge of English. As he spoke, a yellow dog that had been warily regarding the group and snuffing the air suspiciously, uttered a frightened ki-yi, and tucking in its tail, started off as though it had been kicked.

"Your honorable parents are at Mr. Nambo's," observed

the gentleman, who was bowing nearly over, with his body in
a bent position, holding his tall hat with both his hands. "I
hope you will live a thousand years and will always enjoy good
health."

Then he marched off, followed by his wife, who, as she walked, swung her costume in a very Western fashion.

Fitz smothered his merriment until they were out of sight, after which he laughed heartily, and exclaimed, —

"I thought I should have died when she wished us a 'hop-eye nose-ears.'"

"She does not slaughter English worse than we used to Japanese," said Johnnie. "Isn't that so, Oto?"

MODERN JAPANESE.

The young doctor smiled and replied, —

"Yes, you used to mangle 'the language of the gods' pretty badly."

The boys found the house filled with visitors, among whom were the Professor and Mrs. Jewett, many of Oto's college chums, and a number of medical students and government officials; nearly all of whom had been educated in America.

"Good news!" said O-Kiku, as the boys joined her and Sallie. "Professor Jewett has accepted the Chemical Chair in the Imperial College for three years, and after the holidays Sallie is going home with me."

"Rah!" exclaimed Fitz. "Won't we have some jolly times?"

"Yes," answered Johnnie. "visit all the places of interest in the city, and learn how porcelain is manufactured, and how they make Indian-ink, silk goods, fans, and lacquer-ware. We have not half seen the wonders of this great city."

"You must come to Nikko and stay with us," said Sallie. "O-Kiku says Nikko is next to Paradise."

"What mischief are you plotting now?" merrily inquired the Professor, advancing with his wife. "Are you aware, my sons, that you will not see home for three years?"

"We know all about it, sir," replied Johnnie. "Fitz and I are delighted with the prospect. We mean to pass the time in exploring the wonderful city of Tokio."

OWARI (THE END).

www.ingramcontent.com/pod-product-compliance
Lightning Source LLC
Chambersburg PA
CBHW022018240426
43667CB00042B/930